BizPlan Builder 10

BizPlanBuilder® Express 3rd edition

A Guide to Creating a Business Plan with BizPlanBuilder®

JIAN TOOLS FOR SALE, INC.

20 Sunnyside Avenue, A #333
Mill Valley, CA 94941
http://www.jian.com

Burke Franklin

•

Jill E. Kapron

•

Edited by
Jim Reidel

SOUTH-WESTERN
CENGAGE Learning™

Australia • Brazil • Japan • Korea • Mexico • Singapore • Spain • United Kingdom • United States

SOUTH-WESTERN
CENGAGE Learning™

BizPlanBuilder® Express: A Guide to Creating a Business Plan with BizPlanBuilder10, Third Edition

Jill E. Kapron, Jim Reidel, & JIAN Tools for Sales, Inc.

VP/Editorial Director: Jack W. Calhoun

Senior Publisher: Melissa S. Acuna

Executive Editor: John Szilagyi

Sr. Developmental Editor: Emma F. Guttler

Sr. Marketing Manager: Kimberley Kanakes

Sr. Marketing Communication Manager: Jim Overly

Production Project Manager: Stephanie Schempp

Technology Project Editor: Kristen Meere

Web Coordinator: Karen Schaffer

Sr. Manufacturing Coordinator: Doug Wilke

Cover Designer: Tippy McIntosh

Editing and Production: Jim Reidel, d.b.a.

Cover: Cover images courtesy of JIAN Tools for Sales, Inc.

For product information and technology assistance, contact us at **Cengage Learning Customer & Sales Support, 1-800-354-9706**

For permission to use material from this text or product, submit all requests online at **www.cengage.com/permissions**
Further permissions questions can be e-mailed to **permissionrequest@cengage.com**

Library of Congress Control Number: 2006903708

ISBN-13: 978-0-324-42118-7 (package)
ISBN-10: 0-324-42118-4

ISBN-13: 978-0-324-42116-3 (core book)
ISBN-10: 0-324-42116-8

ISBN-13: 978-0-324-42117-0 (CD)
ISBN-10: 0-324-42117-6

South-Western Cengage Learning
5191 Natorp Boulevard
Mason, OH 45040
USA

Cengage Learning is a leading provider of customized learning solutions with office locations around the globe, including Singapore, the United Kingdom, Australia, Mexico, Brazil, and Japan. Locate your local office at **www.cengage.com/global**

Cengage Learning products are represented in Canada by Nelson Education, Ltd.

To learn more about South-Western, visit **www.cengage.com/southwestern**

Purchase any of our products at your local college store or at our preferred online store **www.cengagebrain.com**

Printed in the United States of America
3 4 5 14 13 12 11

The avenues always are waiting. monstrous good is waiting.

—*Delmore Schwartz*

Preface

This third edition of *BizPlanBuilder® Express* has been updated to give you a quick, hands-on introduction to the **full**, interactive Windows version of JIAN's acclaimed software program, BizPlanBuilder 2006 (ver. 10), now with 17 years' worth of refinements built into the **CD-ROM included with every new copy of this book.**

This new edition also does what the very first did: help you learn to create a concise and effective plan for your business, big or small. In this edition, however, you will be able to utilize the full-featured BizPlanBuilder program, which is integrated with Microsoft Office's powerful word processor and spreadsheet applications, Word and Excel, versions 2000, XP, and 2003.[*]

Investors will grill you on everything. As an entrepreneur—or a business student who will one day be an entrepreneur—you will need to seek funding for your startup business venture ranging in size from an "eBay store" to a healthcare network. You will also need to explain your business plan to an investor, banker, venture capitalist, and the like. Most importantly, you must be comfortable discussing every aspect of your business and your business plan. And if you already have a business, you will need to seek funding for expansion, which often requires an "intrapreneurial" business plan and the same preparation and process that goes into a new business's plan.

Managers and owners will grill you on everything. In many businesses today, team leaders and department managers are preparing business plans. Owners and managers want a clear picture of your strategies for success. You may have to define the mission, vision and strategy of your group within the larger organization. And you may have to persuade management to invest in your team and your initiatives. Whatever your needs, *BizPlanBuilder Express* and BizPlan-Builder 10 give you the tools to begin and format a complete, professional business plan in a professional-looking, assembled document.

Now you have a tremendous head start. The process of developing your plan with *BizPlanBuilder Express*, BizPlanBuilder, and the online tools that JIAN makes available will enable you to generate a unique plan and be comfortable discussing anything about your business. Your marketing and sales strategies will substantiate your financial projections—making the difference between a "blue sky" proposition and a viable business venture worthy of a solid investment.

■ Let's Get Started

If you do not have a business concept yet, your instructor will direct you in the selection of a venture that you can use to test-develop a business plan

---

[*] Consult Appendix C, System Requirements for more details and for using BizPlan*Builder* 10 with the Macintosh operating system.

project to learn the process. *BizPlanBuilder Express* provides background information, instructions, assessments—and a hands-on approach to navigating BizPlanBuilder's document templates and resources for preparing each section of your business plan. This text and BizPlanBuilder lead you through the thought process and writing process for each section of your plan. Every document has the language and format you need. All you need to do is provide the words, numbers, and particulars in place of the "variables"—example text and placeholders that you can use or customize.

Part 1, **Business Plan Basics**, is a reality check on writing business plans. It has years of wisdom crammed into a few pages, and it makes a lot of sense. Included in this section are the Top 20 Questions you're most likely to be asked about your business. Be sure to read Part 1 before starting in on your plan. This part also provides you with the first of many hands-on exercises (BizPlan-Buildercises) that familiarize you with the BizPlanBuilder program environment.

Part 2, **Types of Business Plans**, was introduced in the second edition and is expanded here. This part discusses the kinds of business plan master templates that can be used or adapted with BizPlanBuilder, namely concept plans, service/bank loan plans, retail business plans, plans for securing an "angel" or venture capitalist, and Internet business plans. There are also specialized templates designed in conjunction with Cisco Academy for establishing a Cisco-accredited networking academy business.

This part also provides a gradual introduction to BizPlanBuilder new and more secure user interface.

Part 3, **Writing the Narrative**, has a section about the standard nonfinancial components of the business plan, including:

- Title page
- Table of contents
- Vision and mission
- Company overview

- Product strategy
- Marketing analysis
- Marketing plan
- Operations

Each section has background information, instructions, and assessments for that component and any related components of the plan.

Part 4, **Completing the Financial Plan**, has information and instructions for developing your business' financial plan in Excel. In addition to general financial advice, there is also an introduction and survey of the spreadsheets provided with BizPlanBuilder.

Part 5, **Assembling the Plan**, discusses the process of actually assembling your business plan using BizPlanBuilder's automated features. It even includes a hands-on trial run assembling a sample business plan created in earlier hands-on exercises. This part also includes advice about funding and presenting your business plan.

In addition to the main parts of *BizPlanBuilder Express,* the new edition features appendices that cover preplanning your business plan, managing your

▶ **Do It in BizPlanBuilder**

Look for these "Do in Biz-Plan*Builder*" tips throughout *BizPlanBuilderExpress.*

business, BizPlanBuilder's system requirements, where to get training for using Microsoft Word and Excel, a bibliography, and an index.

Internet Access

Take a look at the JIAN website. You'll find a variety of useful information including new products, demos, listings of professional advisors, and links to complementary products and services. Just navigate your Web browser to **http://www.jian.com**—or use the completely redesigned interface for Biz-PlanBuilder 10 that provides context-sensitive access to JIAN's online resources with one mouse-click.

Using *BizPlanBuilder® Express* in the Classroom

The best way for you to progress through *BizPlanBuilder Express* is to create your own real-world company, product, or service (a brewpub, a publishing company, the list is endless) and complete a business plan that puts your vision into words and numbers. Your instructor can direct you in the selection of a company that you can use to model and develop a business plan project that (1) you can see yourself running and (2) realistically could be launched at the end of the semester. The learning objectives, review questions, and activities throughout the book are designed to help you build your knowledge as you prepare to build your plan.

■ JIAN Tools for Sales, Inc.

What is a JIAN? You might think of it this way: while a Black Belt is a master of the martial arts, a "Jian" is a master of every art—the ultimate human with extraordinary acumen, power and resourcefulness. JIAN's mission is to provide strategic building blocks to help managers build better companies—faster, easier and more economically.

Founded by Burke Franklin in 1986, JIAN (jeé-on) began operations as a provider of sales and marketing brochures and direct mail vehicles. Two years later, it introduced the revolutionary BizPlanBuilder software, winner of Success Magazine's "Editor's Choice Gold Medal Award" and *PC Magazine*'s Best Buy rating. BizPlanBuilder, the flagship of JIAN's line, provides business and marketing plan templates for organizing and financing a business. Now the most popular business plan software ever, BizPlanBuilder has sold nearly twice as many copies as any competitive product. Now, with its new high-performance Multi-User Interactive Document Assembly System (MIDAS), BizPlanBuilder provides the latest content as well as the finest Windows and Internet collaborative interface.

All JIAN packages are developed and refined by experts with successful, real-world business experience. JIAN has gathered input from these specialists as well as commissioned accountants, consultants, lawyers and other experts for further guidance. Most of the people at JIAN, as well as the consultants and independent contractors who work for JIAN, are or have been owners of small companies. All of these materials, insights and experience have been engineered into tools and templates you can use to build your business.

Contents

A sensible man never embarks on an enterprise
until he can see his way to the end of it.

—Aesop

Part 1: Business Plan Basics

When there is little or nothing "in writing" about a business's structure, future direction, or position in the marketplace, it is hard to take that business seriously. That is why a business plan is the most important document that you will ever write—next to your success story!

Simply stated, a business plan is a written document detailing the operational and financial aspects of a company. Like a road map, it helps determine where you are, where you want to be, and how you are going to get there—and even how you intend to "close down shop." If it is well written, your business plan will keep you in touch with your goals, potential risks, and probable rewards. Moreover, the plan may be the crucial factor in convincing investors or company management to give you the financing you will need to realize your dream.

Whether you are seeking a loan, looking for an investor, soliciting management, or simply using the business plan to manage your business growth, the ideas outlined in this first part of *BizPlanBuilder Express* provides some useful advice that you will see again throughout this course and in the Biz-PlanBuilder program itself.

This process requires a great deal of research and preplanning. Luckily, however, this text and the BizPlanBuilder application that accompanies it will streamline much of actual composition of the finished plan.

Part 1 includes:

- Why Write a Business Plan?
- Parts of a Business Plan
- Targeting Your Business Plan
- 10 Steps to Complete Your Business Plan
- Top 20 Questions
- Open BizPlanBuilder and Sign in

▶ **Learning Objectives**

After Completing Part 1, you should be able to:

1. Understand why you should write a business plan
2. Know major components of a business plan
3. Determine who the targets of your business plan will be
4. Know the 10 steps to complete your business plan
5. Know the 20 Questions that help you identify your business
6. Open MIDAS, sign-in, and use the BizPlanBuilder startup interface

■ Why Write a Business Plan?

A plan makes it easy to let your banker or other investors in on the action—as well as any other stakeholder in your venture. By reading or hearing the details of your plan, he or she will have real insight into your situation if the bank is to lend you money. Likewise, potential investors can review your plan to gain a better understanding of your business and to determine if their investment is worth the risk.

A plan can be a communications tool when you need to familiarize sales personnel, suppliers, and others with your operations and goals.

A plan can help you develop as a manager. It can give you practice in thinking about competitive conditions, promotional opportunities, and situations that are advantageous to your business. Such practice over a period of time can increase your ability to make wise decisions.

A good business plan saves you money and time by focusing your activities, giving you more control over your finances, marketing and business objectives. But most importantly, for the startup venture, it makes you verbalize—but into words—what would otherwise be ideas and dreams about what your business will be.

What Kind of Plan Is Best for You?

1. A **complete business plan** is necessary when you need a significant amount of funding. You will need to explain your business concept in detail to potential backers, strategic partners or potential buyers of your company. BizPlanBuilder can create and manage all the components of this kind of plan.

2. A **summary business plan** is a shorter format that contains the most important information about your business and its direction. A summary plan is great when you're in a hurry. It is usually about 10–15 pages long and is perfect for many bank loans, or simply to gauge investors' interest. A summary plan is also good for attracting key employees or for convincing friends and relatives to invest a few thousand dollars. This can be done in BizPlanBuilder, too, by carefully selecting and editing the right BizPlanBuilder templates from its master library files.

3. An **operational plan** is the internal document for an ongoing business. It is excellent for focusing the talents of key managers toward a common goal, and therefore should be updated at least annually. A good operating plan can do wonders for any executive's career. This plan, too, can be built by selecting the right templates in BizPlanBuilder.

■ Parts of a Business Plan

▶ **Do It in BizPlanBuilder**

Drop-down list with master plan selections.

Concept Plan
Service/Bank Loan
Retail Plan
Angel/VC Plan
Internet Plan
Cisco Academy Plan

BizPlanBuilder has six master plans from which you can create your own custom business plan. The **Concept Plan** is designed to present a business venture before it is formally expanded into an actual business plan, which is more detailed and includes financial information. The **Service/Bank Loan**, **Retail Plan**, **Angel/VC Plan**, and **Internet Plan** are, as you can readily see, tailored to particular kinds of businesses. (This version of BizPlanBuilder includes templates for designing a specific business plan—a Cisco Academy for teaching computer networking, which is not covered in this text.) The parts

▶ Do It in BizPlanBuilder

The following business plan templates (i.e., narrative parts) sections are included in the Angel/VC plan.

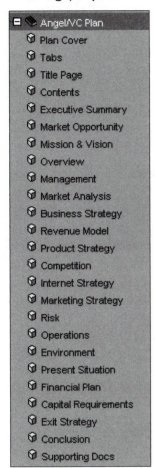

of these plans differ. However, they share many of the same sections and a brief review and description of the most typical are given below.

Plan Cover and Title Page

The title page of your business plan is required and provides the name, address and phone number of the company and the CEO or his or her equivalent. A plan cover can also be used to insert a photograph of your product, someone your performing service, or your proposed logo to catch the eye of an investor or lender.

Contents

The Contents includes a sequential listing and pagination of the sections of your business plan.

Executive Summary

The Executive Summary is a synopsis of your business plan that summarizes the highlights of the plan.

Vision and Mission

This is a snapshot of the present stage of your business, plus a picture of where your business is going and what it will look like, and the goals and objectives on how to get there.

Overview

This section provides basic information about your company: structure, management, staffing, and strategic alliances.

Product/Service Strategy

This section reviews your current product or service and what makes it unique and competitive. Your future research and development plans and production and distribution are part of your product strategy.

Market Analysis and Plan

These sections help you define your market, the demographics of your target customers, competitors' products or services, and business and environmental risks as well as sales, advertising, promotion, and public relations strategy.

Operations

This new section answers questions about business locations, staffing, order fulfillment, returns, and the like. Information technology (IT) should also be covered here—that is, your company's "technology stack," the hard- and software that runs storage devices, databases, application servers, e-commerce, e-mail, and back-office services, and so on. This section is relevant for everything from a very large company to an eBay store operated from your home.

Financial Plan

Your company's capital requirements and the profit potential are analyzed and demonstrated here, and it consists of a narrative and supporting spreadsheet data.

Exit Strategy

This template is where you explain how you would get out of—or "harvest"—your business, such as an IPO or attracting a strategic buyer acquiring companies such as yours. In this section you also describe how repayment will be handled, how investor equity will be converted to cash, and the like.

■ Targeting Your Business Plan

A business plan could be the perfect tool for you to reach the following target audience.

- Associates—to establish agreement, direction and purpose
- Bankers—to provide loans for equipment and expansion
- Business Brokers—for selling your business
- Employees—to align their efforts with yours and keep the vision of your company alive
- Investors—to supply cash for growth, including "angels" and venture capitalists (VCs)
- Marketing Managers—to develop detailed marketing and sales promotion plans
- Small Business Administration (SBA)—to approve low-cost business loans
- Senior Executives—to approve and allocate company resources
- Stock Offerings—to help write a prospectus for selling stock or partnership units
- Suppliers—to establish credit for inventory and materials
- Talented People—to persuade them to join you
- Yourself—to collect your thoughts, analyze your business, set goals and make decisions

Your Reader's Perspective

In addition to providing a large amount of data, your personality and spirit and those of your management team—even if that team, for now, is just you—must show through. You are attracting interested people who can help you. The tone and credibility projected in your business plan will determine their response—how your reader will perceive you and your business and take action ($) on that perception. Remember this and be prepared.

Investors are often heard telling one horror story after another about a business plan "stubbing its toes" on its way into their office. One opportunity is usually all you will get to demonstrate your competence and the feasibility of your project to your investors, senior executives, or clients. These are influential and powerful people. Do not waste their time, bore them, or leave them feeling dissatisfied with your work. Show them that you know what you are doing. Think in terms of return on investment. Show that you can project your company's earnings. Show that you can execute your plan.

Are Your Financial Projections Believable?

Many people think a set of financial projections is a business plan. Numbers sometimes lie or can be used to distort the facts. Most experienced financial people know that a financial projection, no matter how honest and forthright it is, does not represent the complete picture. Conversations with bankers, investors and customers have emphasized how important it is to include several key points in your business plan:

- The state of your market

- Your product or service description in detail

- Market strategy

- Promotion and sales plans

- The management team responsible for using the capital and driving your business toward success

All of this information provides credibility for your financial projections.

Nevertheless, the financial plan demonstrates the viability of your business, whether it is a startup or an established company. Review your financial plan indicating your projected performance. Rethink your strategy, make changes and see the results . . . and be able to explain your plans.

Different financing sources look for different things and emphasize different areas—you must be prepared for all of them. Refer to Funding Resources for Your Plan in Part 5. It discusses where to find the money that is *right* for you and your business, and that makes the difference between success and failure.

■ 10 Steps to Complete Your Business Plan

Depending upon your experience and time, you may choose to read the instructions and advice for each section of your business plan before actually creating each section using the BizPlanBuilder application.

Here's a suggested procedure for using *BizPlanBuilder Express* to write your business plan:

1. For a "warm-up" exercise, begin by answering the Top 20 Questions that begin on page 6. The answers to these questions will form the foundation of your business plan. They will also help you to pick the right preplanning documents in Appendix A, Preplanning Resources in BizPlanBuilder.

▶ **Do It in BizPlanBuilder**

File-tree list with document templates in the Pre-planning masters folder.

⊟ 🗐 Pre-planning
　🗐 About BizPlanBuilder
　🗐 Business Assessment
　🗐 Executive Team Bio
　🗐 Personal Assessment Questions
　🗐 Personal Mission Statement
　🗐 Writing About Your Business
　🗐 Investor Tracking
　🗐 LLC Operating Agreement.doc
　🗐 Sample Term Sheet
　🗐 Vision

2. After reading Part 2, Writing the Narrative, do a fairly quick first draft on the templates for each section. (You may want to edit the Title Page, Table of Contents and Executive Summary after completing your second draft.)

3. Follow up with research on areas for which you did not have sufficient information while doing your first draft.

4. Read Part 4, Completing the Financial Plan, and then prepare your supporting financial statements using the BizPlanBuilder spreadsheet templates. Fill in the worksheet for the financial portion of the business plan.

5. Use the applicable BizPlanBuilder templates to prepare a word-processed draft of the entire business plan. Fill in the gaps in the first draft of the plan as you go. Complete your Title Page and Table of Contents, Executive Summary and Supporting Documents. Include documents as needed. This is the second draft.

6. Have several trusted people look over your second draft for questions and their recommended changes. This includes legal and accounting professionals, too. The latter are especially important given Sarbanes-Oxley Act (SOX) compliance. If your IT requirements and architecture will be sophisticated, consider specialized IT consultants as well.

7. Input any useful changes to your draft and do a final edit of your business plan. Use at least two people to independently edit/proofread your plan.

8. Input final changes. Read Assembling Your Plan in Part 5 before final printing and distribution of your plan.

9. Identify your target audience and include both a nondisclosure agreement and cover letter with your plan.

10. Distribute and track your plan through phone calls, letters, and via email as needed.

■ Top 20 Questions

Originated to help develop advertising brochures and promotional pieces, the **Top 20 Questions** are what most people will ask you about your business. The responses can be used before you use BizPlanBuilder's preplanning tools discussed in Appendix A. (This book, of course, and BizPlanBuilder will help you develop and enhance your responses further.)

1. What type of business do you want to build?

_____

_____

_____

_____

_____

2. What is the purpose of your business?

_____

_____

_____

_____

3. Who are your target customers?

_____

_____

_____

_____

4. What is your primary product or service?

_____

_____

_____

_____

5. What is the primary function of your product or service?

_____

_____

_____

_____

6. What are three unique benefits of your product or service?

_____

_____

_____

_____

_____

7. What is your reason for being in this business? (What's a nice person like you doing in a business like this?)

_____

_____

_____

_____

8. What led you to develop your product or service?

_____

_____

_____

_____

9. Who is your competition?

_____

_____

_____

_____

10. How is your product or service different from that of your competition?

_____

_____

_____

_____

11. What is the pricing of your product or service versus your competition?

_____

_____

_____

_____

12. When will your product or service be available?

_____

_____

_____

_____

13. Is this product or service used in connection with other products/services?

_____

_____

_____

_____

14. Are you making any special offers to distributors or customers?

_____

_____

_____

_____

15. What is the key message or phrase that describes your business?

_____

_____

_____

_____

16. What are your current plans for advertising and promotion?

_____

_____

_____

_____

17. Do you have datasheets, brochures, diagrams, sketches, photographs, related press releases, or other documentation about your product?

_____

_____

_____

_____

18. How will you finance the growth of your business?

_____

_____

_____

_____

19. Do you have the management team needed to achieve your business goals?

_____

_____

_____

_____

20. How do you intend to get out of your business when it's a success?

_____

_____

_____

_____

■ BizPlanBuildercise 1.1: Open BizPlanBuilder and Sign in

► Do It in BizPlanBuilder

See Appendix C, System Requirements for BizPlan-Builder, for installation procedures. Also see the **Hand-book of Planning.pdf** file in the JIAN folder on your Biz-PlanBuilder CD-ROM. Adobe Acrobat is required to view this document.

The following steps and the steps for the BizPlanBuilder exercises in this book are designed for the interactive version of BizPlanBuilder for Windows. See Appendix C if you use Macintosh and adapt this exercise

Before you begin, you must have BizPlanBuilder 10 and the MIDAS™ Multi-User Interactive Document Assembly System engine installed on your PC. The installation wizards are automatic. Simply insert your BizPlanBuilder CD-ROM and when the onscreen Flash movie window opens, click the appropriate installation options. (You may also click to see the QuickTour slide presentation and the Intro Video, which will introduce you to BizPlan-Builder's many features.)

During the course of the MIDAS installation wizard process, you select the Share Your Plan option so that you can access your plan from other computers. This setting will also be useful for classroom instruction, where your classmates and instructor can have access to your plan for review.

If you have selected to launch BizPlanBuilder after you click **Finish**, you can skip step 1 below.

Part I. Start BizPlanBuilder

When you start BizPlanBuilder, you will see a reminder to access the JIAN website to automatically activate your copy of BizPlanBuilder 10. You can only start the program seven times before activation is required. Student users who purchase the printed edition of this textbook should use the instructions and any serial number supplied in the inside cover.

1. In Windows, click **Start**, **All Programs**, **Jian**, then click

    OR

    Click the **JIAN** desktop shortcut.

2. In the MIDAS login dialog box shown below, click the **New User** button if this is your first time launching BizPlanBuilder or if you are adding someone other than yourself as a new user.

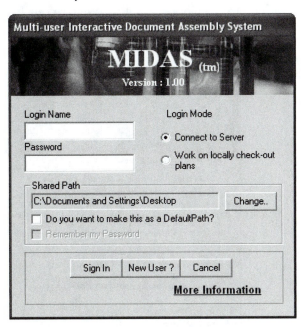

3. In the User Addition Form dialog box shown below, type your desired user name and password in the appropriate text fields and click **Add**.

User Name		🐾
Password		
Retype Password		

> ▶ **Do It in BizPlanBuilder**
>
> Consult your instructor about installing any free demos offered on your installation CD-ROM. Their features are beyond the scope of this text.

4. In the login dialog box, type your newly added user name and password in their text fields.

5. If desired, select the **Remember my Password** option.

6. Click the desired Login Mode option. In this example, click **Connect to Server**.

7. In the Shared Path field, your Windows desktop is the default path. You can click **Change** and navigate to another location. In this example, the default is selected.

> **See "Moving the Business Plan Folder from the Desktop" in Appendix C for additional instructions and consult with your instructor if your Plan Folder needs to be in another location.**

8. Click **Sign In**.

9. The BizPlanBuilder icon tutorial window opens. You can click on these buttons to view BizPlanBuilder's online resources. This same button array is available as a toolbar in the BizPlanBuilder window. For this exercise, click **Next**. *Hint::* If you don't want to see this window each time you login, deselect the **Always show this screen at startup** option.

10. The JIAN Professional Network window opens. For this exercise, click **Next**. *Hint::* You can also deselect the **Always show this screen at startup** option.

11. .In the Choose the Purpose of Your Plan wizard dialog box (shown below), read the introductory text and then select the **Choose your plan type form the MIDAS Master Plans** options.

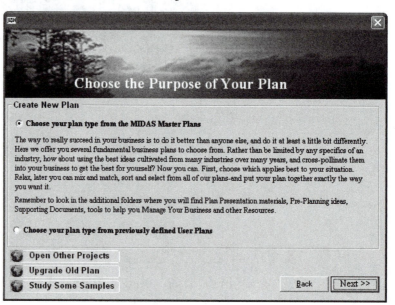

12. Click **Next**.

Part II. Review BizPlanBuilder Master Plans

In the second part of this exercise, you will review the different plan templates that you can select from the Choose the Purpose of Your Plan wizard.

1. In the second dialog box of the wizard shown below, select **BizPlanBuilder** from the Select Product list.

2. The dialog box is populated with BizPlanBuilder's base plan options as shown below.

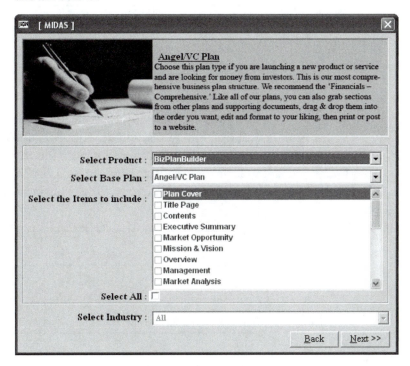

3. Click the **Select Base Plan** list arrow.

4. Notice there are selections for Concept Plan, Service/Bank Loan, Retail Plan, Angel/VC Plan, and Internet Plan—the four major business plan categories—as well as the Cisco Academy Plan.

5. Click **Concept Plan** and read accompanying explanatory text next to the graphic.

6. Repeat steps 2 and 3 for each type of plan.

7. For this exercise, you will click the ☒ button. In subsequent exercises, you will begin to develop a sample business plan in BizPlanBuilder.

■ **Review Questions 1.1**

1. What is a business plan? Why should someone in business or thinking of going into business write one?

_____

_____

_____

_____

_____

2. Molly LeDier is starting a home-office based company that offers "prepress" services such as copyediting, proofreading, and even "page-making" textbooks, brochures, and other publications. She has a partner and they intend to gradually grow their business and to relocate to an office closer to their client base when their business, LogaTorial, is established. Who might be the key targets for the PartyWorks business plan?

_____

_____

_____

_____

_____

3. Ozark Welding Supply is a 25-year-old company that delivers welding gas, rods, and wire to manufacturers and repair shops in a 100-mile radius. The owners have decided that they want to add a retail outlet to serve people with welding equipment at home or the very small business. What financing source would you suggest? What kind of business plan (complete, summary, or operational) should they develop?

_____

_____

_____

_____

_____

_____

4. How will answering the Top 20 Questions that may be asked about your business assist you in completing your business plan?

_____

_____

_____

_____

_____

_____

_____

_____

_____

_____

■ Activities 1.1

1. You should have a business concept in mind that you will use throughout this workbook. If you are not at that point yet, you can "adopt" Molly LeDier's LogaTorial concept—or another fictional business. (Consult with your instructor first.) After you have selected a concept, work through the Top 20 Questions.

2. Look at the section 10 Steps to Complete Your Business Plan (see page 5). For each step, estimate hours or days to complete. Build a time line. How long do you estimate it will take to complete the ten steps?

3. Now that you have read the master plan descriptions in BizPlanBuilder, consider which plan best suits your own entrepreneurial interests. Write down the type of plan—Service/Bank Loan, Retail Plan, Angel/VC Plan, Internet Plan. Do not rule out a Concept Plan, which you can use to formally "sketch" out your business. Let's see if that choice holds true at the end of this course.

Ideas are the beginning points of all fortunes.

—Napoleon Hill

Part 2 looks at the different types of business plans and their associated templates in BizPlanBuilder. This part also tells you how to choose the right one. To learn more about BizPlanBuilder's updated interface, the Concept Plan is used as a starting point and example of how to navigate a typical BizPlanBuilder Masters template.

Part 2: Types of Business Plans

This part covers the:

- Concept Plan
- Service/Bank Loan Plan
- Internet Plan
- Retail Plan
- Angel/VC Plan

- Financial Documentation
- Additional Resources
- Selecting a Plan in BizPlanBuilder
- Open (and Delete) a Plan

▶ **Learning Objectives**

After Completing Part 2, you should be able to:

1. Understand the different business plan templates
2. Understand the supporting documentation and resources
3. Select a business plan template and enter basic data
4. Open and navigate a BizPlanBuilder template
5. Open, close, and delete a plan in BizPlanBuilder

■ Business Plan Types

There are four basic business plan masters in BizPlanBuilder: the Concept Plan, Service/Bank Loan Plan, Retail Plan, Angel/VC Plan, and Internet Plan. (You can examine the Cisco Academy plan on your own.) Except for the Concept Plan, each plan has document templates and sections in common—and templates that are specific to the business type for which each plan is designed. Not every template is covered in this book. Nevertheless, Part 3 uses the Service/Bank Loan Plan as a representative example and the discussion, wherever possible, will alert you to the relevant differences and provide information for completing the other plan types because each business venture is as different and diverse as the businesspeople and investors who make them possible.

The Concept Plan: An Executive Summary

The concept plan is designed to help the entrepreneur think through many of the details needed for writing the actual business plan. The concept plan can be used in-house, or it can be circulated informally to friends, associates, mentors, or others who can offer constructive advice. Typically, however, it is a way of getting your ideas on paper for the first time. The Concept Plan helps to:

- Evaluate your concept
- Identify areas where you need to do some research
- Suggest ways to approach the necessary research
- Think through how you want to approach certain aspects of your business
- Explore options you hadn't originally considered

Because your business concept may be for a service, technology, or product that does not exist yet, the concept plan template is designed as a series of questions and research ideas—literally the homework and grunt work that results in the finished business plan and financial models. The Concept Plan is an overview and a foretaste of the process you will need. The template provides you with a structure for entering the information that your research yields. This same process will used again to build the actual business plan.

The Executive Summary

When you are done with your Concept Plan, BizPlanBuilder creates a printout with the title page Executive Summary. This alerts potential investors to identify your concept as an investment opportunity. This section will ultimately become the mini-version of the entire business plan and its development here ends as the Executive Summary in your formal, expanded, and finished business plan.

It is everything summarized in one to three pages and its purpose is to generate excitement. So, as you massage and revise it, from its very beginning in the Concept Plan, make sure you create a clear, compelling, detailed discussion of your value proposition.

> The Concept Plan template is shown in the figure below. The bracketed areas—called *variables*—are for information that you supply. Click the **Next Variable** button ⊖ to move from one variable to another to customize the boilerplate example text. Variables are used in virtually all BizPlanBuilder plan templates.

> **Concept**
> This concept grew out of [a long-standing thought that xxx / the belief that a (person/business/organization) should be able to xxx or xxx / desire to create xxx / frustration with the only available xxx / the inconvenience associated with xxx / the costs associated with obtaining xxx / having to travel to xxx to get xxx / etc.].
>
> LogaTorial [is creating an / will launch an / has an established] operating infrastructure, with [well-recognized brands / customer letters of intent / proprietary content / satisfied business communities /strategic partners / distribution channels / outsourced production]. LogaTorial is now transforming its products and services, as well as its fundamental business model, to take full advantage of [the newest Internet-based technologies /current market trends / recent changes in xxx].

Service/Bank Loan Plan

This type of plan template is designed for those starting or building up a preexisting small or personal service business for which a bank loan is the typical method of financing such a venture. Previous versions of BizPlanBuilder offered a separate Product Plan. If your business is product-oriented and relatively modest in scope—for example, you sell or make stuffed collectible animals, custom build computers, and so on—you can easily modify this plan.

The Service/Bank Loan Plan template is especially tuned for the sole-proprietor .An example would be a freelance textbook editor, a business consultant, a desktop publishing service, an accountant, a truck driver, and the like. Such businesses may include one or more staff members, in addition to the owner/founder, so there can be a staffing dimension to this kind of plan. Though these professionals typically do not seek outside financing and start with a lower initial investment—indeed, sometimes the investment is no more than their talent and a home office—the Service/Bank Loan Plan is ideal for the next step—seeking a bank loan. You can add elements from the other plan models and various kinds of supporting documents. Depending on your business opportunity's complexity, a Basic or Financial Model—Intermediate is recommended.

> **Business plan templates have onscreen *Expert Comments* in a light-green comment font as shown below. These prompts and tips do not print when you generate the final business plan in the Interactive version of BizPlanBuilder.**

❖ Use this page to design a nice cover for your plan

❖ Use a photograph of your product or of someone performing your service – replace our logo below.

❖ This of this as a cover of your brochure – make it attractive to an investor or lender.

LogaTorial

Your slogan here

> **Expert Comments are also featured in BizPlanBuilder financial templates.**

	A	B	C	D	E	F
1	This worksheet shows who gets how many shares, when and what you think they'll be worth.					
2	Stock Give-Up... Be careful about giving up too much. How much before you lose your motivation? Investors need you to be					
3	Your team must be motivated. Everyone very motvated. Don't let anyone take that away from you.					
4	Use the information learned from the Valuation Summary & Investor Analysis pages.					
5	Despite the valuations calculated on the previous page, you will likely want to enter your own Price / Share here.					
6	Remember, you may not need or use all of these financing rounds -- HIDE the columns you won't use. (Likely, E,F and/or G)					

Retail Plan

The retail plan is designed for retail stores in neighborhoods, malls, cities, and in other fixed or even mobile locations. It can be retail, catalog, online, home-delivery, office-delivery, roadside, vending machine route, and the like. It can be a storefront business that offers walk-in shopping, delivery service, online collateral and contact options, online ordering, and combinations of these.

The retail plan, unlike the service plan, features components that larger operations such as chain and department stores require, including an executive summary, marketing strategy, a more detailed analysis of customers, competition, and management for more than one employee. Financial models that demonstrate the viability and expected profitability of this kind of business play a significant role in this kind of plan. Depending on the size of your venture, BizPlanBuilders' Intermediate and Comprehensive Financial Model templates, specially designed Microsoft Excel workbooks, can be used for this part of your plan.

Internet Plan

The Internet Plan template is designed for businesses that are predominantly on the Web. The size of the business can be small, sole proprietorships or large-scale operations with sizeable staffs. For example, such a business plan can be used for an online store or catalog operation, an Intranet service provider, an information service offering news and advice, a Web-hosting company, an interactive educational presentation service, and the like.

If the Internet is part of a larger business better suited to one of our other plan types, you can still cut and paste sections from this plan type and customize another plan later. The same financials apply to this plan as with retail plans.

Angel/VC Plan

The Angel/VC (for Venture Capitalist) Plan is the newest business plan template package offered in BizPlanBuilder 10. It is specifically designed for presenting your business idea and financials to venture capital and angel investors. This plan can be tailored for a new or expanding product- or service-oriented business that is looking for money from investors.

For this kind of plan, targeting your audience is crucial. So are detailed financials. However, an economy of length is needed for your audience is composed of busy men and women who have a limited amount of time to weigh your opportunity against others. The final length should be no longer than 30 pages—which is the 8 oz. limit for a standard FedEx or UPS next-day letter. However, the Angel/VC businesses plan you prepare is also your "script" for answering the battery of question that demanding investors will throw at you before they ever write you a check. Details and supplementary documentation should be in place for quick access and ready answers.

■ Financial Documentation

The spreadsheets necessary for various financial considerations to project how much money you need to start your business venture are prepared separately from the business plan narrative. Your company's profit potential is also analyzed and demonstrated here—and for that reason it is recommended that these spreadsheets be prepared professionally by your accountant for every kind of business. This is especially true given new, post-Enron accounting legislation such as the Sarbanes-Oxley Act. Only the smallest, sole proprietorships can get away with do-it-yourself number crunching!

For small businesses, BizPlanBuilder provides a Microsoft Excel workbook that includes a basic balance spreadsheet, cash flow projection sheet, income statement, and, importantly, a service startup sheet. With the advice and assistance of your accountant, you can input these numbers.

For larger and more complex businesses, BizPlanBuilder provides Intermediate and Comprehensive Financial Models that are best prepared by your accountant with full sharing privileges. These templates are discussed in detail in Part 4, Completing the Financial Plan.

■ Additional Resources

BizPlanBuilder is a feature-rich application when it comes to added resources to prepare the groundwork for your business plan, write it, and submit it to banks and potential investors. There is even a resource for *running* your business after you have your funds. There are four Masters categories: Pre-Planning, Plan Presentation, Supporting Documents, Manage Your Business, and specialized Resources. These materials are too many to discuss in any detail here. However, the brief descriptive review that follows will give you an idea of their extensive scope:

- **Pre-planning**, for example, contains tutorial documents for assessing your business, writing about it, preparing a team biography, writing a personal mission statement, setting up an LLC, and so on (see Appendix A).

- **Plan Presentation** has tutorial documents for writing a cover letter to a banker, an angel investor, sending out an email announcement, making an elevator pitch, and the like (see Part 5).

- **Supporting Documents** has templates and tutorials for supplying a range of materials that might be needed to augment a business plan, such as an executive team resume, a list of core practices, and personal finances statements (see Part 5).

- **Manage Your Business** shows you how to apply for business credit, exploit free publicity, the Lehman Formula Calculator, and other documents, templates, and utilities (see Appendix B).

- **Resources** contains articles on what investors are looking for in a business venture, developing a management team, creating money highlights and so on (see Part 5).

■ BizPlanBuildercise 2.1: Select a Plan and Supply Basic Information

Part I: Select a Plan

For this exercise you will create a sample concept plan to print out and examine.

1. Launch and sign-in BizPlanBuilder. (See BizPlanBuildercise 1.1 if necessary.)

2. In the Choose the Purpose of Your Plan dialog box, click **Choose your plan type from the MIDAS Master Plan**s option if necessary.

3. Click **Next**.

4. Select **BizPlanBuilder** in the Program list.

5. Click **Concept Plan** in the Select Base Plan list.

6. Click the desired parts of the plan. For this exercise, even though there is one part, click the **Select All** option check box.

7. Click the **Next**.

8. In the User Information Form, type the name of your plan in the Plan Name text box.

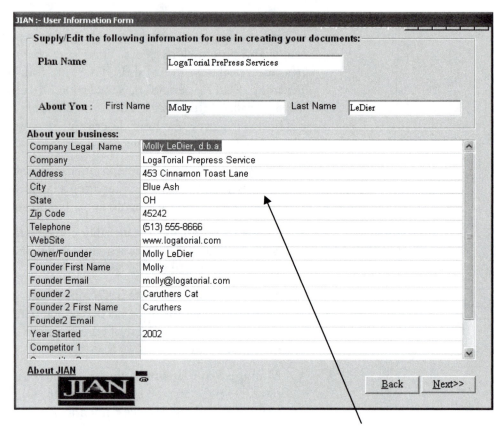

9. Type the desired basic information as shown in the illustration. You can substitute your own name, address, and other personal information in place of the sample data or use the sample data for this exercise.

10. Click **Next**.

11. The Grant Access Permissions dialog box appears (shown on next page). For each user, select the desired sharing privilege using the drop-list besides each name or the all-users buttons that apply permission globally:

      a. No Access

      b. Read

      c. Full Control

12. Click **Finish**.

The BizPlanBuilder window appears.

Select users sharing privileges in the Grant Access Permissions dialog box.

Grant Access Permissions

Plan Name :   **LogaTorial PrePress Services**

User Name :   **molly ledier**

Grant Access Permissions

System Users	Permissions
admin	Full Control ▼
james reidel	No Access
	Read
caruthers	Full Control

No Access All	Read All	Full Control		Finish

Part II: View the BizPlanBuilder Window

The BizPlanBuilder window is divided into two panes. The **Item List** on the left is divided into two sections organized into file trees. The upper white portion is the [User Name's] Active Plan section. This is where the current business plan is displayed (with an open-book library file icon 📖. It can be expanded to show a closed-book library icon ◆, which, in turn, can be expanded to show a file tree and the component documents (both selected and unselected) for the current plan.

The lower portion, which is dark gray, shows nonactive templates and documents that you can access, such as Shared Plans, BizPlanBuilder Masters, which are attached to the file tree under a bookshelf library icon 📚. In this portion of the Item List, you will find the templates for the different kinds of business plans—shown as closed-book library icons—as well as the other documentation and resources available to supplement a professional business plan. This lower portion is also where you can select Other User Plans—also represented with a bookshelf library icon—which contains the Cisco Academy business plan suite that ships with BizPlanBuilder 10.

1. If necessary, expand the Active Plan in the Item List by clicking the + sign and then double-click 📦 Business Concept Plan .

2. A warning appears that informs you about using Save-As to save documents in another location. You should use the automatic saving system as described. Click **OK** to continue. (You can hide this message in the future by clicking **View** in the BizPlanBuilder menu bar and then clicking **Hide Double Click Message**.)

3. Notice that Microsoft Office launches in BizPlanBuilder's **Document pane** to the right of the Item List and the Concept Plan document opens.

4. Study the BizPlanBuilder file window in the left pane and the Word document pane on the right.

5. Notice that for the Word document to be active, you must click in that window, making sure that title bar is active (blue) and not inactive (gray). (See the figure below.)

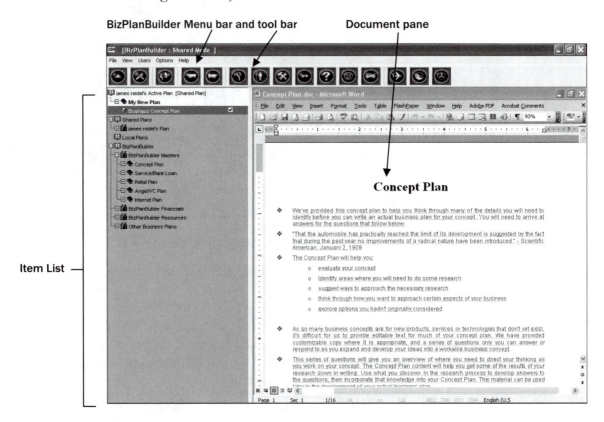

6. Scroll through the document with your mouse.

7. Then return to the beginning of the document.

8. Find the BizPlanBuilder window toolbar shown below.

9. Rest the mouse pointer on each icon and read the ScreenTip that identifies each button's function. Locate the following and when you do place a check mark in the box provided.

- Start A New Plan ☐   - Previous Variable ☐
- Assemble Plan Preview ☐   - Next Variable ☐
- Show/Hide Expert Comments ☐ - Back up Plan ☐

10. Click the **Next Variable** button until the following variable is selected:

Overall, our company can be characterized as a **retail merchant / computer hardware installation, service and repair / wholesale deli and bakery / childcare / car rental** business specializing in [your area of specialization].

11. Replace the first variable by typing **prepress services**.

12. Click the **Next Variable** button and replace the variable about your area of specialization with **college textbooks.**

13. Click **File** and **Save** from the Word menu to save changes to your document. *Caution:* If you do not save as you would normally do while working on an office document, your changes will not be preserved.

14. Click the **Next Variable** button to go to the next variable. Click several times and study each variable.

15. Click the **Previous Variable** button to navigate back to any unedited variable.

16. To print the Concept Plan, click the **Print** button on the Word toolbar.

17. To close BizPlanBuilder, use the menu command.

18. Click **File** and then **Exit**.

19. If asked to save, click **Yes**.

■ BizPlanBuildercise 2.2: Open (and Delete) a Business Plan

▶ **Do It in BizPlanBuilder**

To open a different plan from the Other User Plans and make it the current plan:

1. **Expand the file tree.**

2. **Right-click on the desired plan.**

3. **Then select it as the Active plan in shortcut menu.**

Because you can rarely finish an entire business plan in one BizPlanBuilder session, you will frequently need to open and close your plan again as you finalize the finished document. Sometimes, you may also need to delete documents in the plan—even an entire plan—as well as rename items and the like..

In this next exercise, you will reopen the plan you created in the previous exercise and delete it.

Note: By default, BizPlanBuilder saves your files in a Business Plan folder on your Windows desktop. For the duration of this course, be careful not to move or delete this folder. Consult the manual that came with your copy of BizPlanBuilder and with your instructor about changing the location of this folder.

1. Launch BizPlanBuilder and sign in.

2. Click 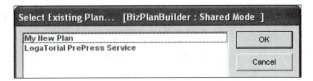 in the Choose the Purpose of Your Plan dialog box. The Select Existing Plan dialog box opens shown below.

3. Select the desired plan and click **OK**.

4. Click **Next** in the User Information Form dialog box.. *Hint:* You can make changes here that will be applied to your plan automatically. For example, if

you need to change the business name, type the new name in the appropriate text field.

5. In the BizPlanBuilder window Item List, double-click the desired plan document. In this exercise, select the sample **Business Concept Plan** you created in the previous exercise.

6. If a warning window appears, click **OK** to continue. The Concept Plan opens in the Document pane.

Delete a Plan Document

1. Right-click the document in the BizPlanBuilder window Item List.

2. Select **Delete** in the shortcut menu. A dialog box appears asking you if you are sure you want to delete.

3. Click **Yes** or **No** as desired.

Delete a Plan

1. Right-click on the plan's name or library icon in BizPlanBuilder window Item List. For this exercise, select the **LogaTorial Prepress Service**.

2. Click **Delete** in the shortcut menu. A dialog box appears asking you if you are sure you want to delete.

3. Click **Yes** or **No** as desired. For this exercise, click **Yes**.

■ Review Questions 2.1

1. Which master business plan would be used by a sole proprietor of a vending machine route? What about a vending machine franchise company?

_____

_____

_____

2. Which business plan would be most suited for a chain of hair salons that offered their own line of hair care products?

_____

_____

3. Which business plan is most suited for designing websites? Which is most suited for a hosting them?

_____

_____

4. You are first-time entrepreneur. What is the advantage of preparing a concept plan, even if you already know what kind of business you want to start?

_____

_____

_____

■ Activities 2.1

1. Read the Concept Plan printout created in BizPlanBuildercise 2.1. On a separate piece of paper, write in as many possible variables for the kind of business plan you have in mind.

2. If you do not have a business plan in mind yet for the above activity, create a fictional one—you might use the brewpub example, which is both a service and a product business—and address the variables. List them and write out or discuss the kind of information that you would need to supply for each entry. (This activity can also be performed as a class activity.)

3. Start BizPlanBuilder. In the Choose the Purpose of Your Plan dialog box, click [🌐 Study Some Samples] and examine the sample assembled business plans that shipped with your copy of BizPlanBuilder.

4. To see a plan with the narrative and financials, repeat the steps in Activity 2 and view the Hilltop Bed and Breakfast sample business plan.

*My aim is to put down on paper what I see and what I feel
in the best and simplest way.*
—*Ernest Hemingway*

Part 3: Writing the Narrative

Part 3 introduces the nonfinancial pieces of your business plan puzzle. These make up the **narrative**. BizPlanBuilder masters offer five kinds of plan narratives—Concept, Service/Bank Loan, Retail, Angel/VC, and Internet—each of which has sections in common or unique to the business type in question. For this reason, we look closely at one plan, the Service/Bank Loan Plan, to learn the basics for creating the plan narrative—skills that can be used for working with the other template masters.

We also survey the important features and sections of other master plans that are appropriate for their business venture type. Because any business plan is really a customized production, think in terms of using templates that might not be found in the BizPlanBuilder master that you start out with (e.g., you may be better off with a Vision and Mission statement from the Internet master).

This part covers the following:

- Plan Cover/Title Page
- Contents
- Executive Summary
- Company Overview
- Market Strategy
- Operations
- Conclusion
- Relevant BizPlanBuilder skills for adding users, permissions, entering text, adding templates, and more.

▶ **Learning Objectives**

After Completing Part 3, you should be able to:

1. Create the narrative part of your business plan
2. Understand the importance of having a formal title page and contents
3. Understand the function and components of the Executive Summary
4. Understand the important role of the company overview section
5. Strategize your market—define your market and profile your customers and your competition
6. Describe the operations—the human resources—of your business
7. Learn about other kinds of plan components
8. Locate and open applicable templates in BizPlanBuilder

■ Plan Cover and Title Page

The Plan Cover is a newer feature in BizPlanBuilder. Use this cover sheet like the cover of a book—as a place to put your business plan's title and a visual, such as a logo, a photograph of someone performing your service or product. You can also insert a slogan, a blurb, or other short statement that supports your plan. The Plan Cover is not required, so you can delete it in the Item list.

The Title Page of your business plan should always begin with your company name, address, and phone number. In addition, your Title Page should contain the name, address, and phone number of the CEO (Chief Executive Officer). This also means the sole proprietor in a small business plan.

If your plan is distributed to several investors or bankers, you should include a special copy number discussed later. This identification number will allow you to track the plans and limit the circulation to the intended audience. Keep a list of who received your business plan and when, and do appropriate follow-up by phone or mail.

Your plan should also include a confidential and proprietary statement as well as a disclaimer regarding securities. Boilerplate language is provided for these in all master plan Title Page templates.

Because BizPlanBuilder is automated, the information that you typed in the User Information Form dialog box is used to fill in some parts of the Title Page when you first open it in the Document pane.

The BizPlanBuilder window with Title Page open in the Document pane.

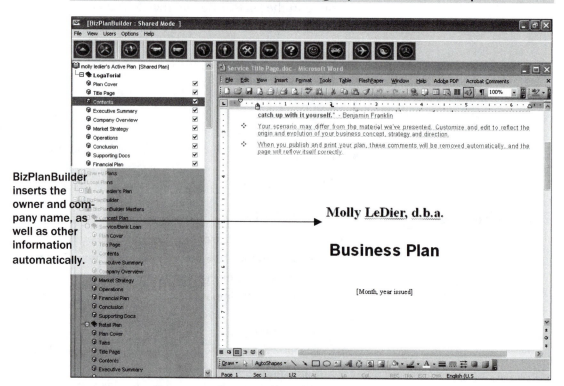

BizPlanBuilder inserts the owner and company name, as well as other information automatically.

To edit the title page (or cover page) in Microsoft Word, right-click the item in the Current Plan file tree and select **Open** or double-click it. If you see a warning message about saving your documents, click **OK**. Remember, you can click **View** and **Hide Double Click Message** to suppress these warnings if they become an annoyance.

The check mark option boxes next to each current plan component in the Item list indicate that the document is active—and part of your current business plan. The lack of a check mark means that the document is inactive and not included in the plan. You can make a document active (or inactive) by right-clicking on it and selecting **Set Active/Inactive**. You can also click a document template's check box to select or deselect it.

■ Contents

The Contents provides a quick reference to the key documents of your business plan. It lists each one and has placeholders for their page numbers. These may startle you at first—especially if you are new to Microsoft Word—because they are marked "Error! Bookmark not defined." Don't worry, these placeholders are changed to sequential page numbers automatically by the BizPlanBuilder engine when you click the Assemble Plan Preview button on the BizPlanBuilder toolbar and save the finalized plan discussed in Part 5, Assembling Your Business Plan.

Also, somewhat disconcertingly, you will notice that the items listed in the unassembled table of contents differ from those selected in current plan. Only the items that are selected as active in the current plan appear in the finalized Contents.

> **In Microsoft Word you can set up your final plan into sections and apply section-numbered pagination (e.g., as 2-1 to 2-7) instead of the automated straight sequential numbering used by the BizPlanBuilder application. You can also reset the automated table of contents feature to reflect this kind of numbering. Consult Microsoft Word's help feature (Press F1). Also see Appendix D, Using Microsoft Word and Excel.**

■ Executive Summary

The business plans of most enterprises require an Executive Summary. This is even true now for sole proprietorships. Although your business plan begins with the Executive Summary, it is the last component—and the most important section—you will finalize. It provides you with the opportunity to make a strong first impression on your target audience.

Function of the Executive Summary

The Executive Summary template— Executive Summary —in BizPlanBuilder serves two important functions. First, it should convey to the reader that you have an accurate understanding of your business. It is like the "hook" in a good novel. It should compel the reader to continue on to obtain a fuller picture of your company. If it does this, then the rest of your plan will have a chance to stand on its own merit.

Second, due to time or other constraints, the Executive Summary may be the only section of your plan that some evaluators read first. How good it is determines whether they read the rest. If you assume that your reader may have only five minutes to review your plan, what are the most important points to convey?

All things considered, the Executive Summary should be brief (one to three pages) and should contain highlights of your company, its products, its markets, and its financial position and performance—both current and projected. Including knowledge of your industry, management team and financial reports, as well as your plan to pay back investors, will convince your reader that your business can and will succeed. Most importantly, the Executive Summary explains your experience and role in the business—and how you will make it a success (or have made it a success if your plan is designed to seek funding for expansion).

Parts of the Executive Summary

The Executive Summary briefly discusses each component of your business plan. Depending on the BizPlanBuilder template that you use, these components typically include mini-versions of, for example, the Company Mission, Market Opportunity, Customer Base, Store Location, Industry Trends, Service (or Product) Strategy, Business Model, Management Team, Capital Requirements, Projected Revenue tables, Business Risk, Exit Strategy and Return on Investment, and other summaries that correlate with the components of the plan you choose—as well as a Conclusion. Obviously, the Executive Summary is your sales pitch to investors. (These, of course, can serve as the outline to a Power-Point presentation that complements your business plan. See Part 5, "Making Your Presentation.")

Selected components are discussed in depth throughout the rest of this part *BizPlanBuilder Express*. It is recommended that you complete each section of your business plan before writing the Executive Summary. However, you can always enter information you have to any business plan template before you assemble and finalize your final business plan—BizPlanBuilder allows you to systematically work on your plan-in-progress.

Executive Summary Checklist

√   Have you written all of the other components of your business plan? (If you haven't, you shouldn't begin writing the Executive Summary.)

√   Does your Executive Summary convey to the reader that you have an accurate understanding of your business?

√   Does your Executive Summary compel the reader to continue on in order to obtain a fuller picture of your company?

√   Does your Executive Summary cover the most important points of your business plan?

√   Does your Executive Summary contain highlights of your company, its products, its markets, and its financial position and performance—both current and projected?

√   Does your Executive Summary contain knowledge of your industry, management team and financial reports and discuss your plan to pay back investors?

√   Is your final copy of the Executive Summary one to three pages in length?

■ BizPlanBuildercise 3.1(A): Add New User, Give Sharing Rights, and Create a Business Plan

In this exercise you will add a new user, give yourself and that user sharing rights, and then create a Service/Bank Loan Plan.

> **When instructed to "Launch BizPlanBuilder" from this point, it means to open MIDAS and, if applicable, selecting BizPlanBuilder as the desired program.**

1. Launch BizPlanBuilder.

2. Click **New User?** in the MIDAS login dialog box.

3. In the User Addition Form dialog box, type in **Caruthers** or a fictional name of your choice in the User Name field and then type a password in the other two appropriate fields shown below. Your password must be between 6 and 15 characters in length.

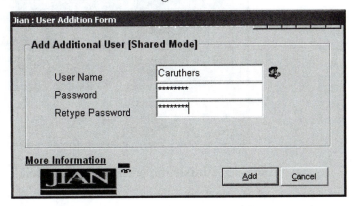

4. Click **Add** and the **OK** to close the thank-you message.

5. In the MIDAS login dialog box, type the user name and password that you created in BizPlanBuildercise 1.1 into their appropriate fields and then click **Sign In**. Do not sign in with the new user name you created in step 3.

6. Click **Next** if needed to open the Choose the Purpose of Your New Plan wizard dialog box.

7. Click **Choose your plan type from the MIDAS Master plans**.

8. Select BizPlanBuilder as the desired product if necessary and then select the **Service/Bank Loan** plan and click **Select All**.

9. Click **Next**.

10. In the Info for Plans dialog box, type the name of your plan in the Plan Name text box. In this example, **LogaTorial Prepress Services** has been entered.

11. The information you entered in BizPlanBuildercise 1.1 should appear in the other fields of the Info for Plans dialog box. If not, reenter the appropriate information.

12. Click **Next**.

13. In the Grant Access Permissions dialog box, select **Caruthers** (or the name you entered in step 3) under System Users and select **Full Control** from the Permissions drop-down list.

*Note: To grant the same permission type to all users, click the **No Access All**, **Read All**, and **Full Control** buttons as desired.*

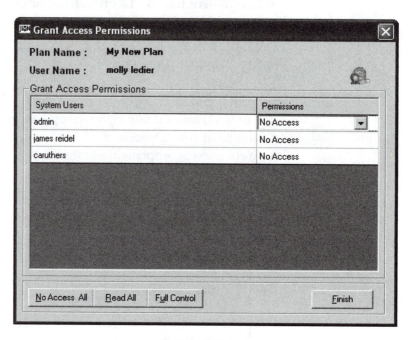

14. Click **Finish** and go on to BizPlanBuildercise 3.1(B).

■ BizPlanBuildercise 3.1(B): Navigating a Template and Entering Text

▶ **Do It in BizPlanBuilder**

Click on the window frame as shown, hold down the mouse button, and drag the right pane to the left.

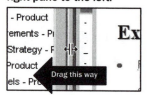

In this exercise you will open the Executive Summary template, examine its content, and enter text.

1. .In the Item list, double-click 🔘 Executive Summary for the current business plan in the Item list.

2. Click **OK** to close the warning window if necessary.

3. Maximize the BizPlanBuilder window and drag the right pane to the left to almost cover the left pane. This will make it easier for you to read and edit the document without having to scroll right or left.

4. Notice the bulleted list that describes the purpose and content of the template. Read the items in the list.

5. Scroll down to the heading **Company Mission**.

6. Let's say you are Molly LeDier and you can already decide on some of the wording and articulate the purpose of your company as you review the paragraph under Company Mission. If desired, you can also substitute your own wording that best expresses the kind of business plan that you want to build.

   a. Point and click the mouse after the heading Company Mission in order to place the insertion point there.

b. Click the **Next Variable** button in the BizPlanBuilder toolbar to select **[was / will be]** and press **Delete**.

c. Delete the unnecessary words, spaces, and characters to change **[established / introduced]** to **was established**.

d. Click the **Next Variable** button.

e. Change the following text. **[describe the purpose for your company's existence]** for **[customer / client business type]** in the **[locale / market / industry]** to **professional prepress services under the name LogaTorial Editorial Services** for **publishers** in the **college textbook industry.** Press the **Next Variable** button as needed to move to each variable as you edit.

f. Press the Next Variable button to select **[describe the highest priority characteristics of your service]** and edit to read as **manuscript-to-bound-book results.**

The result is the draft paragraph illustrated below.

Company Mission

Molly LeDier, d.b.a. was established in 2002 to provide professional prepress services under the name LogaTorial Editorial Services for publishers in the college textbook industry. Drawing on our own experience, the resources at our disposal, and the expertise of others, we strive to provide our clients with the best possible manuscript-to-bound-book results in a timely manner, and with the greatest possible attention to the details that support their success, and their satisfaction with our service.

---

7. Scroll through the remainder of the Executive Summary and read the BizPlanBuilder help tip for each section.

8. When you are finished, close BizPlanBuilder and click **Yes** when asked to save the business plan.

■ Review Questions 3.1

1. Why should the title page include a copy number?

_____

_____

_____

_____

2. BizPlanBuilder automatically numbers your business plan consecutively. Would you use that method—or the Contents pagination style that has section numbers followed by page numbers within each section? Why?

_____

_____

_____

_____

_____

_____

3. What is the purpose of the Executive Summary?

    _____

    _____

    _____

    _____

    _____

    _____

4. Carlos Martin wants to write a business plan for a mobile accounting service. He begins by writing his Executive Summary. Is this a good place to begin? Why or why not?

    _____

    _____

    _____

    _____

    _____

    _____

5. Answer this question after you perform BizPlanBuildercise 3.1(B): Identify the components of the Executive Summary for the Service/Bank Loan Plan and list those that might appear in your business plan.

    _____

    _____

    _____

    _____

_____

_____

_____

_____

_____

_____

_____

■ **Activities 3.1**

1. Set up a sample plan cover and title page for your business concept.

2. Perform this activity after you finish BizPlanBuildercise 3.1: Copy and paste three or four sections into a separate Word document and try to edit them to match up with a business plan that you might write. At this point do you have all the information that you need? Print your results.

> **You can perform this activity while still in the BizPlanBuilder Document pane. Just click the New Document icon and Word will open in a new window outside of the BizPlanBuilder window.**

A person to carry on a successful business must have imagination.
He or she must see things as in a vision, a dream of the whole thing.
—*Charles M. Schwab*

Nothing ages so quickly as yesterday's vision of the future.
—*Richard Corliss*

Vision and Mission: Expressing the Company Direction

The essence of a business plan is to define and communicate what your company is today, where it is headed in both the short and the long term, and how the company is going to get there. Whether you are promoting and describing your existing company, a company concept or a product concept, the principles outlined in this section will apply.

No matter what the size of your venture is, even if you are a sole proprietorship, you should consider adding a narrative about your Company Direction. It should explain to your reader why you are in business and what you intend to achieve. You should express your present position, even if you are only in the planning stage. This statement can introduce or be worked into a statement that covers your vision of the future, your mission, and your present situation that should ensure your reader about your will and expertise to accomplish your goals. BizPlanBuilder makes this possible because you can customize your business plan by including a Mission & Vision Statement when you begin your plan or add it later from the Master templates—the dark gray area—in the Item list. You can even add and adapt a Mission & Vision Statement from one master template (e.g., Internet Plan) and insert it into a plan that lacks such a template (e.g., Service/Bank Loan plan).

Also discussed in this section is the Present Situation component, which can be related to vision and mission and may need to be drafted at the same time.

■ Looking at the Big Picture

▶ Do It in BizPlanBuilder

Add a business plan template part to the current (open) plan, (1) click the expand arrow next to the desired business plan template in the right pane of the BizPlanBuilder window: Then (2) right-click the desired part icon and choose **Add to Current Plan**.

All activities of your company should be in alignment, aimed in a certain direction. Your business may seem like this sometimes, and at other times activities may seem scattered. When writing your business plan it is crucial to know what your company is today, where it is headed in both the short and the long term, and how management is going to make sure the company gets there. This is the essence of planning.

If you are writing your business plan to outline, promote and fund a specific company concept, a product concept or a new product line, rather than for an entire existing company, the same principles outlined here will apply, although not on as global a basis. If this is your situation, you may not need to put as much time and detail into this section of your plan.

Just as important as defining your direction, you must be able to clearly communicate these concepts to many people (employees, partners, vendors, customers and potential investors) in the course of growing the business.

How well this communication works affects whether the success potential of your business will be realized.

It is critical on both accounts that these words be put into writing. The work and care you invest into this component of your business plan will form a backdrop for subsequent components. Your plan will thus have a focus and be easier for your target reader to visualize.

■ Vision Statement

By defining and understanding your company's future destination you help determine the feasibility of your business' success. Vision is simply a picture of where your business is headed. It describes the dream, the intended future destination of your business, based on realistic long-term projections of the present situation. It puts into brief words what the company will be like, how big it will be, what industry it will be serving, what kind of products it will be providing, and who future customers will probably be. The vision for some businesses may be described in terms of a few years into the future, while others in more mature and less volatile industries describe vision in terms of 10 to 20 years or more into the future.

The Vision Statement can influence a wide range of people. Potential investors, employees and potential employees, partners, vendors and customers can all contribute to drive your company to success . . . if they buy into your vision. Your business plan needs to help facilitate this *buy-in*.

Putting Vision to Words

There are dangers in creating long, grand, or abstract visions for a company. These visions are less believable, only vaguely understood, and most difficult to communicate and attain. The Vision Statement should be reality-based and should not paint a larger picture than the company has a good chance of growing into. If the vision is clearly achievable, rather than self-serving fluff, you can more readily develop a concerted team effort and build enough momentum to make it happen.

Being too idealistic, too, can be counterproductive. For example, using a buzzword term such as "stakeholder" too much—or and in the wrong way—can be a dead giveaway that you are not focused on making a profit.

It is advisable for the owner, founder, or leader of your company to take the first pass at writing a Vision Statement. After all, this is where the vision probably began. It should be shared with key members of senior management (and, if applicable, with the board of directors) for feedback and fine-tuning. If the company and concept is embodied in one person—you—then it is important for you to be your best critic, to ask yourself: Would I believe my own vision if I heard it for the first time and from someone else?

The Vision Statement should lay out a path for your company to stretch its possibilities, yet it must remain simple, believable, achievable, and understood. All people involved in and associated with your company should be able to comprehend and in some way relate to the vision. Otherwise your company and its management "may wind up making more poetry than product," as a senior manager once aptly proclaimed. It is still the wisest vision of all to provide real products and services that real people will buy!

■ Mission Statement

Your company's Mission Statement should concisely describe, in writing, the intended strategy and business philosophy for making the vision happen. In a few sentences it conveys how all the combined efforts put into your business will move it toward its vision. It should distinguish your business from all others. Mission statements can and do vary in length, content, format, and specificity.

Fred R. David, a prominent strategist, gives the following components and corresponding questions that a Mission Statement should answer. [*]

1. **Customers.** Who are and who will be your customers?

2. **Product.** What are your company's major products or services?

3. **Markets.** Where does your company compete?

4. **Technology.** What is your company's basic technology?

5. **Concern for survival, growth, and profitability.** What is your company's commitment toward economic objectives?

6. **Philosophy.** What are the basic beliefs, values, aspirations and philosophical priorities of your company?

7. **Self-concept.** What are your company's major strengths and competitive/technological advantages?

8. **Concern for public image.** What is your company's public image and standing in the community?

9. **Concern for employees.** What is your company's attitude toward its employees?

Depending on the size and complexity of your business, you may feel that only a few of the above components need to be directly addressed in order to produce an effective Mission Statement for your company.

Some companies communicate their mission in only a sentence or two. As an example, the one-sentence version of JIAN's Mission Statement is as follows:

> JIAN's mission is to be the preferred source for comprehensive, innovative software, products, services and resources that enable business people worldwide to build, maintain and enhance their businesses successfully.

Other companies use a couple of paragraphs or more to detail their Mission Statement. Whatever the length or format of their statement(s), every word should count. A Mission Statement should be both highly descriptive

---

[*] Source: Fred R. David, *Strategic Management* (Columbus, OH: Merrill, 1989).

and inspirational. It should be broad enough to cover a range of strategies and objectives, while calling attention to the top priorities.

A Mission Statement, even more than a Vision Statement, should be a team effort. It should accurately reflect the operational direction and spirit of your business. If the Mission Statement is not supported by the various managers and departments within the organization, then it may well be inaccurately or incompletely reflecting the true direction of your business. For a reality check, your Mission Statement should be revisited regularly, at least before the annual planning or budgeting process.

Need for Written Statements

Many business people dismiss the need for written vision and Mission Statements, considering the process as mere linguistic exercises with little or no impact on the real workings of the business. However, many studies and informed sources indicate that companies (and individuals) with written vision and Mission Statements have a far higher success rate than companies that do not. Conversely, the vast majority of companies that fail have not had written vision and Mission Statements.

■ Goals and Objectives

Goals and objectives translate thought into action. The difference between goals and objectives is that a goal is the level of achievement you must to attain to reach your mission. An objective is the specific measurable action that achieves the goal itself. Together, they focus people and activities. Achievement is meaningful if the reason for achieving matches what is important. The *Wall Street Journal* showed a survey of the top goals for Americans in the '90s. The breakdown was as follows:

- Spend time with family and friends: 77%

- Improve themselves intellectually, emotionally or physically: 74%

- Save money: 61%

- Have free time to spend any way they please: 66%

- Make money: 61%

- Travel or pursue other hobbies or personal experiences: 59%

Businesswise, goals must align with the big picture of your company. This section of your business plan provides information on the business goals that will be achieved as your company operates according to its Mission Statement on the way toward reaching the stated vision of its future.

Business Goals

While the Mission Statement conveys how your company will conduct its business, the goals state which accomplishments will need to take place to move the company in the direction of its vision.

Goals must measure a predetermined level of performance to be achieved within a specific time period. Each major business goal should be tied into the long-range plans of the business. It should be written in a manner that supports the company's Mission Statement. As an example, suppose that your mission stated that your company was to become the manufacturer of the highest quality widget on the market. An aligned goal might be worded as follows:

> In order to become the manufacturer of the highest quality widget on the market, defective products returned by customers will be less than 1% for the year.

Each specific objective should be written so that the goal that it is supporting is expressed. Goals should focus on getting results by making the organization work more effectively. Goals serve as a contract between people and build responsibility, accountability and growth. Consistently setting and attaining appropriate goals is an indicator of a business person's ability to define and run his or her business. Well thought-out and supported goals in a business plan indicate to the audience that the business is on the right track:

- Deal with vital issues
- Contribute to profit or productivity
- Are measurable and specific
- Tie into company vision/mission
- Are stated as end results
- Offer challenge but are realistic
- Are controllable by you
- Are time limited
- Are rational
- Provide a return on investment
- Have financial objectives
- Position the business for growth

For the majority of businesses, there are many basic goals an owner might choose to adopt. The following is only a sample of what an entrepreneur has to choose from.

- Market Penetration
- Market Maintenance
- Market Expansion
- Diversification
- Utilization of Capacity
- Specific Net Profit Percentage

- Profit Maximization

- Asset Productivity and Return on Equity

Methods for Building Goals

A good way to begin setting goals for your business is with sales and marketing goals. The first stage is goal-based on the bare minimum dollar value of sales your business must reach to break even based on expenses you have researched and expect to incur. Once you have completed those calculations based on expenses, you can compare your "must reach" break-even sales level with demographic studies to determine if the target market has enough demand. The Market Analysis and Opportunity section later in Part 2 discusses demographics further.

Using this same strategy, you can set your next goal to earn a specific Return on Investment (ROI) by a certain date, you can test it by comparing your required profit to your projected sales. An example would be if you used $10,000 of your own money to start the business and you want to earn a 20% return on that investment. This means you would have to break even plus earn a $2,000 profit. Again, you can compare this projected sales volume to the demographics to determine if the market has sufficient demand.

You can take this approach and use varying expense amounts based on different locations, different capital requirements based on those different locations, and varying returns on investment. By doing projections this way, you are able to compare various locations and return on investment requirements that you have established as goals. Instead of trying to set an arbitrary sales figure, you can set concrete goals and then determine if the market can support those goals.

In preparing these projections by month and for future years, also consider any seasonal fluctuations in sales, the effect of inflation on your expenses and sales prices, and any debt repayment you might have on borrowed money. For further discussion on projections, see Part 4, Completing the Financial Plan.

If you have an existing business, these projections are a little easier to prepare. You can base your expense projections on actual expenses your company has incurred, rather than on researched estimates, and you can base your sales goals on past sales growth performance. You can use the same techniques as a new business if you want to set specific return-on-capital requirements for your existing business. Instead of comparing these goals with demographics, you can compare them with past performance to see if they are realistic.

■ Present Situation

In the Angel/VC Plan, the master template includes a separate and related component: Present Situation—which can, of course, be applicable to other kinds of ventures. This is the starting point for any discussion of the vision of your future begins with—and the questions to consider are:

- What is your business doing on a daily basis?

- Who is your company serving through its products and services, and how?

- What real benefits or values does your business provide today?

If you have done an honest assessment of your company's overall strengths and weaknesses, you can be more objective in your description of what your company really is, rather than what it should or might have been. Readers of your business plan want to know if you are in touch with the reality of your business situation. After all, it is the business that best works to meet the real needs of its customers over time that will survive and thrive.

After you look at the broad view of your current corporate position, similar questions should be addressed regarding specific areas. In your business plan's Present Situation discussion, briefly (a sentence or two for each area) touch on management, products, product life cycles, market environment, pricing and profitability, customers, distribution, financial resources and any other area you feel is vital. This is your best opportunity to give your target reader an accurate glimpse of your company today.

■ Summary

If a company's vision, mission, and goals are aligned, the company is well on its way to success. If your company is far from this level, do not despair. Well over 99% of companies are in this same situation. The key here is to use the company vision to motivate—thus ensuring your company's long-term success.

■ Vision and Mission Checklist

√ If applicable, what is your company's present business situation regarding products and services, benefits, or values?

√ What is your dream for your company?

√ How large will your company be?

√ What industry will your company be serving?

√ What kind of services or products will you be providing?

√ Who are your current and future customers?

√ Is your Vision Statement reality based?

√ Does your Vision Statement accurately describe the growth that your company can achieve?

√ Has a key member of senior management provided feedback and fine-tuning to the Vision Statement?

√ Does your Mission Statement describe the intended strategy and business philosophy for making the vision happen?

√ Does your Mission Statement distinguish your business from all other similar businesses?

√ Did a team of managers from various departments write the Mission Statement?

√ Are you regularly revisiting your Mission Statement to determine if you are meeting the concepts included in it?

√ Do the goals of your company clearly state the accomplishments that need to take place to move the company in the direction of its vision?

√ Is each major business goal tied into the long-range plan of the business?

√ Are the goals focused enough for getting results by individual organizations?

√ Do you have a sales goal?

√ Do you have a marketing goal?

√ Are your goals appropriate, acceptable, feasible, flexible, measurable, specific and understandable?

■ BizPlanBuildercise 3.2(A): Add a Vision and Mission Statement Template

> **The LogaTorial plan is only an example. Use your own plan if desired and the template that best suits your business. Then adapt the steps with the help of your instructor.**

1. Launch BizPlanBuilder if necessary.

2. Sign in as Molly LeDier or yourself and choose to work on the **LogaTorial** example or your own business plan.

3. Expand the [BizPlanBuilder Masters] library in the gray area of the Item list by clicking the plus sign.

4. Click the plus sign in the [Angel/VC Plan] master library to see all of its template files.

5. Right-click on [Mission & Vision] and click **Add to Current Plan.**

6. Click and hold the mouse button down on the Mission & Vision template and drag it in the list so that it follows the Executive Summary.

7. Release the mouse button. The template that you added to your business plan should appear as shown below:

8. Continue to part (B) of this exercise.

■ BizPlanBuildercise 3.2(B): Review the Vision and Mission Statement Template

1. Double-click [Mission & Vision]. (Click **OK** to close the warning message if necessary.

2. Expand the Document pane as desired.

3. Review the **Expert Comments** at the top of the document.

Vision, Mission, Goals & Objectives

> *"For I dipt into the future,*
> *As far as human eye could see,*
> *Saw the vision of the world,*
> *And all the wonder that would be."*
> - Alfred Lord Tennyson

❖ For an overview of company Vision and Mission, refer to the BizPlan*Builder Handbook of Business Planning*, and the "Vision" and "Personal Mission Statement" resource materials in the Pre-Planning section of BizPlan*Builder*.

❖ You and your staff may want to write both your Vision and Mission Statements completely from scratch. Be sure you capture the spirit and uniqueness of your business.

❖ What is the vision that drove/drives the creation of your business? This is a "big-picture" view of what your business is about, and where you see it in the future. Include what you want for the business and for yourselves (personally and financially) 5-10 years from now.

❖ Your vision should incorporate what you see as your company's role in the world and in the lives of the your stakeholders—customers, employees, vendors, investors, and the environment—everyone and everything you touch or impact.

❖ Expand your thinking on this. Allow yourself to see the biggest possible picture—from 360°.

4. Scroll down to the **Vision** heading. Notice that BizPlanBuilder provides you with additional Expert Comments and examples.

5. Scroll down to the **Mission Statement** heading. In addition to the Expert Comments, the BizPlanBuilder template will offer industry-specific options (if applicable) for filling out certain sections of the template component.

6. Scroll down to the **Goals** heading. This is a fairly detailed section having a number of subsections (Corporate, Market, Products, and so on) depending on the business type. Note the importance of real financial goals. This section should be prepared with an accountant's advice and, in many instances, should not be omitted.

7. Scroll down to the **Objectives** heading. This section is optional and may or may not apply to your business. Because BizPlanBuilder templates are virtually comprehensive, you may need to make decisions about deleting sections that do not apply to your business. Plans for startup businesses and those already established have different needs.

Objectives

❖ Optional: Depending on the target audience you want to reach with this business plan, you may or may not need to include this section on the specific objectives or tactics your company will employ to reach the strategic goals listed above.

❖ If you do not wish to go to this level of detail, delete this section. Otherwise, obtain the required information (from your management team, if applicable) and complete this section.

❖ **Cheat me in the price, but not in the goods.** - THOMAS FULLER

❖ **Real discipline is when you can pick strawberries without eating any.** - DOUG LARSON

❖ Where do you want to go from here? What will an investor's or lender's money buy you? Specifically? What will it look like?

Projected revenues for fiscal year 20[xx], without external funding, are expected to be $[x]. Annual growth is projected to be [x]% per year through 20[xx]. We feel that within [months / quarters / years] LogaTorial Prepress Service will be in a suitable position to [add additional stores in other parts of the city / add additional product lines to xxx / expand our existing facilities…].

8. Return to the top of the document.

9. Close BizPlanBuilder if desired. It is not necessary to save the Vision & Mission document.

■ Review Questions 3.2

1. What portions of the business plan narrate the company's direction? How long should it be?

_____

_____

_____

_____

_____

2. How can a Vision Statement help reveal the feasibility of a business's success?

_____

_____

_____

_____

_____

3. Who should write the Vision Statement? Why?

_____

_____

_____

_____

_____

4. Why should the Vision and Mission Statements be written documents?

_____

_____

_____

5. What is a Mission Statement? How is it different from a Vision Statement?

_____

_____

_____

_____

6. How do business goals relate to the Mission Statement?

_____

_____

_____

_____

7. A firm states that during the third quarter it intends to increase sales by 12% by hiring three new salespeople, calling on 50 new customers, and increasing trade show activity by 10%. Does a statement of this type consist of goals or objectives? Would this statement fit in a business plan?

_____

_____

_____

_____

■ Activities 3.2

1. The writer Delmore Schwartz wrote that in dreams begin responsibilities. With this in mind, answer the question "What is your dream for your business venture?" Do so in three or four sentences and compare your results with your class or with a colleague.

2. Using your own business concept, write a real or hypothesized Vision and Mission Statements (such as one for Molly LeDier's prepress services business). Use the vision and mission checklist starting on page 38 to guide the development of these statements.

Many years ago Anaheim, California, was mostly a giant orange grove,
but Walt Disney saw Frontierland, Tomorrowland, Fantasyland . . .
imagine what it took to explain Disneyland.
—Anonymous

Company Overview

The Company Overview sets the stage for your business plan. This section describes the legal structure of your business. It can be considered simultaneously with the related section for Management, which follows the Company Overview in BizPlanBuilder's template libraries. In the following sections, the Overview component for the Retail, Angel/VC, and Internet business plans is discussed first because it is the most comprehensive and traditional in format.

The Company Overview begins with a brief survey of the business's establishment and purpose—and a longer business description section divided into three primary sections. The first is the legal business description. The second section provides information about the business location or locations. The third section deals with any government regulations that impact the way you do business.

The Company Overview for the Service/Bank Loan plan is different in form and content and discussed separately.

■ Legal Business Description

Company Name

A business is a legal entity and requires a company name that is approved and registered with your local government prior to the opening of a new business. The legal name of your company may be different than the name used in dealing with customers. If you intend to operate under a name other than your own, you must file a Fictitious Business Name statement in order to be "doing business as" (For example:Molly LeDier, d.b.a. LogaTorial Prepress Services). The fictitious business name is usually more descriptive of the product or service. Used with a company logo, the fictitious business name may also promote recognition for your product or service.

The Legal Forms of Business

BizPlanBuilder supports Sole Proprietorships, subchapter S- and C-Corporations, Limited Liability Companies (LLC), Partnerships, and, Limited Liability Partnership (LLP). These comprise the three basic forms a business can take are proprietorship, partnership, and corporation, which will be discussed in this section. Each form has distinct advantages and disadvantages concerning ease of startup, tax considerations and legal liability. In recent years a new hybrid status called a Limited Liability Company (LLC) has become popular in some startup situations. The LLC is discussed later in this section.

Sole Proprietorship

A sole proprietorship is the easiest way to open a business. This form has a single owner and the only legal requirement to establish it is a local business license. Just as easily, you can dissolve or close the business at any time, and it automatically ceases upon your death. As the sole owner, you have absolute authority to make all the decisions.

The major disadvantage of a proprietorship is that you are personally liable for all debts and contracts. There is no distinction between personal and business debts, so if the business cannot pay its bills, creditors can sue to collect from your personal assets. Income from the business flows directly through to you and is taxed at the individual rate. You do not pay yourself a salary; your income is the profits from the business. There is also no carry back or carry forward of losses. Although last year you did not have to pay any taxes because of a loss, this year you will have to pay the full taxes on your profits; you cannot cancel out this year's profits with last year's losses and pay taxes only on the net total for the two years.

Partnership

The second form is the partnership, of which there are two types: general and limited. In a general partnership, two or more people combine money, property, skills, labor or any combination of resources to form the assets of the business. Each partner is a co-owner and is entitled to a share of profits and losses. The percentage of each owner's share is described in the partnership agreement, which is not required, but should exist in writing. It should describe the percent ownership of each partner, the management responsibilities of each, how the profits or losses of each will be distributed, how the owners can withdraw capital or money from the business, how partners can be added to or allowed out of the business and what happens if one of the owners dies. As in proprietorship, there are no legal requirements to open other than local licenses to operate and the Fictitious Name if you operate under a name other than the partners' names. Unless otherwise specified in the partnership agreement, the partnership dissolves immediately upon the death, insanity, or insolvency of any one partner. Again, the disadvantage of the partnership is that every partner is fully responsible for all debts and contracts. Any business obligation entered into by any one partner is binding on all partners, regardless of the amount they invested.

The second type of partnership is a limited liability partnership (LLP), which consists of at least one general partner and one or more limited partners. In a limited partnership, only the general partners have any decision-making authority or any type of input as to the operation of the business. The limited partner contributes capital only and cannot participate in the running of the business. Unlike the general partners who are fully liable for all debts and contracts of the business, the limited partners cannot be personally sued because of the debts of the business. The most that limited partners can lose is their investment, but the general partners can lose their investment and be sued for personal assets. The limited partnership is organized under state laws and certain documents must be filed with the state.

In both forms of partnerships, all income is passed directly through to the individual owners in percentages described in the partnership agreement. The same tax rules as a proprietorship apply with regard to profits being taxed at the individual rate and the taxing of capital gains. However, in a partnership, losses are carried back three years and forward for 15 years. The partnership files a complete return with the IRS, which includes a Form 1065 (a business profit and loss statement). Each individual partner will file a Schedule K-1 and a Schedule E for his or her percentage of the profits.

Corporation

There are two kinds of corporations: a C-Corporation and an S-Corporation. In both, ownership of the company is evidenced by shares of stock, which are readily assignable or transferable (you can use them for collateral on a loan or sell them at any time). In theory, corporations are separate legal entities from the owners. They can open checking accounts, borrow money, and operate just as a person might in the business world. Because of this unique structure, the business continues forever despite changes in ownership or management. Also, corporations offer what is called "limited liability" to the owners, which means the owners cannot be sued for the debts of the business unless they have personally guaranteed those debts. Therefore, the potential loss for you, the owner, is limited to the capital that you invested. (Capital does not have to be money. It can be property, machinery, skill, or labor.) Debtors can sue the corporation only and can claim only the assets of the business. For this reason, banks will usually require most closely held corporate owners to cosign or guarantee any loans.

Ultimate control or management of the company is in the hands of the shareholders, who generally meet once a year and who elect a Board of Directors. The Directors usually meet to oversee major corporate policies. They appoint Officers who hire management to run daily operations. In a small company, the shareholders are also the Board of Directors and management.

In a proprietorship or partnership, the company has only two ways to get new capital: personal money or money borrowed from a bank. A corporation, however, can sell shares of stock, borrow directly from the public by selling corporate bonds or borrow from a bank.

Because a corporation is considered to be an individual identity, it must file an IRS tax return and pay taxes on its profits. Unlike a proprietorship or partnership, profits do not flow directly through to the owners. If the owners are also company employees, their salaries appear as expenses on the company's books and are reported as wages on the individuals' 1040 form. If the company earns a profit after all expenses (including owners' salaries) and the owners want to take that money out of the company, then those profits are paid to the owners as "dividends" and are reported on the individuals' 1040 tax return along with Schedule B (interest and dividend income).

This is one disadvantage of a corporation. Not only are the profits taxed on a corporate basis, but if they are distributed to the owners, they are taxed again at the individual level, creating "double taxation." A corporation shares the same tax advantage as a partnership in that it can carry losses back three years and forward 15 years. These losses are used to offset profits and limit the company's tax payments. If the business had losses last year and did not pay any taxes, you could carry those losses forward to this year's tax return and offset any taxable profits.

To incorporate, a legal document called the "Articles of Incorporation" must be filed with the Secretary of State of your local state. The Articles must include the legal name of corporation that contains "corporation" or "incorporated," how stock is to be issued, corporate governance procedures, and other considerations that are beyond the scope of this book. (See *The BizPlanBuilder v10 Handbook of Business Planning* on your CD-ROM for an expanded discussion of this and other business structure topics.)

An S-Corporation differs from a C-Corporation in regard to a few tax considerations. In order to be an S-Corporation:

- Your company must be domestic.

- There can be only two classes of stock: voting and nonvoting.

- Only individuals may own stock.

- There cannot be any nonresident aliens as shareholders.

- The company cannot own any subsidiaries or be part of any affiliated group of companies.

- There can only be a maximum of 35 shareholders.

An S-Corporation files a full corporate tax return as C-Corporations do (Form 1120), only they use a Form 1120S. However, the return is for informational purposes only. The profits or losses flow directly through to each shareholder based on the number of shares owned.

The shareholder reports profits as supplemental income on a Schedule E. Therefore, not only does the owner report wages on the 1040, but he or she also reports the distribution of profits as supplemental income. The advantage is that the S-Corporation does not pay taxes on the profits and double taxation is avoided. All profits must be passed through to the owners and taxes paid on those profits, even if the owners do not actually take the money out of the business. The final tax advantage is that, unlike the proprietorship and like the C-Corporation, an S-Corporation can carry losses forward or backward to offset previous or future profits. Given these tax considerations, when most people incorporate they do so as an S-Corporation as long as they expect to operate at a net loss. In this way, losses are passed through to the individual owners. However, once the company starts to become profitable and to retain those profits, the S-Corporation election is dropped to prevent taxes on that money retained in the business.

Limited Liability Company (LLC)

During the 1990s, many states began adopting a designation for businesses called a Limited Liability Company. LLCs are a hybrid of the above types, providing tax benefits equivalent to those of a Limited Partnership and protection equivalent to that of a C-Corporation or an S-Corporation. LLCs can be privately held companies only, although they can be changed to C-Corporation status if you want to go public at a later date.

As of the end of 2002, most jurisdictions, including the District of Columbia, have LLC legislation in place. Check with your state government or legal representative to determine if your jurisdiction is without such a law—or if an area you are going to do business recognizes an LLC. Most legal firms make it easy and inexpensive to incorporate such a company, too—some even offer online incorporation via the World Wide Web. At this writing, there are following advantages and disadvantages to this designation:

Advantages of a limited liability company:

- **Limited liability.** Members are shielded from being personally liable for acts of the LLC and its members.

- **Flexible membership and profit distribution.** Members can be individuals, partnerships, trusts, or corporations, and there is no limit on the number of members or the profits they receive.

- **Management.** Members can manage the LLC or elect a management group to do so.

- **No Minutes.** Unlike corporations, an LLC does not have to keep formal minutes of its proceedings.

- **Flow-through taxation.** Income, losses, deductions, and tax credits flow through the LLC to the individual members.

Disadvantages of a limited liability company:

- **One member LLCs.** Many jurisdictions do not allow LLCs to have only one member, although the number of jurisdictions that do allow them is growing. Under federal law, a single-member LLC is treated as a sole proprietorship.

- **Free transferability of interest.** In older LLCs, transferability of interests was usually restricted to enable the LLC to be treated as a partnership.

- **Nontraditional entity.** An LLC is a new entity type for which there is little precedent available.

- **Limited Life.** Corporations can go on forever. An LLC is dissolved when a member dies or goes bankruptcy.

- **Going Public.** It is best to go public (IPO) as a corporation.

- **Complexity.** Again, a corporation is more suited for complex business operaions.

- **Cost.** An LLC usually costs more to form and maintain than a sole proprietorship or a general partnership. States may also charge an initial formation fee and an annual fee; check with your state's secretary of state's office.

■ Business Location

This section of the Company Overview serves two purposes. One, it gives the basic information about where your offices and other facilities are located. It also explains to potential investors and other interested parties how the location of your business plays a decisive role in its success—that is, how you serve your customers. If your locations have not been physically established and require financial backing as part of your vision, consider the following questions to flesh out this part of the Company Overview:

- What are your location needs?

- What kind of space will you need?

- What makes an area desirable? a building desirable?

- Is the intended location easily accessible? Is public transportation available? Is street lighting adequate?

- Are market shifts or demographic shifts occurring?

■ Government Regulations

An increasing concern for investors is how a business, whether established or getting started, stands vis-à-vis the federal, state, and local government. The input of your legal counsel, as much as the advice you get from your accountant, is important when addressing this section and others like it in your business plan. For example, is the land that you want to build on—which you just discussed in the Business Location section—free of soil contamination? Would you be liable for any EPA-mandated cleanup costs? This and major obstacles can exist.'

In this section, discuss how you have dealt with or plan to deal with any legal obstacles and how you intend to meet the "letter of the law" both in your operations, how you intend to report financial information (Sarbanes-Oxley factors here), and whether any government regulations have bearing on your legal business structure. You can also consider:

- The licenses and permits required. Here you may want to include copies in the Supporting Documents section of your business plan.

- How would you describe your company's relationship with the relevant government agencies?

- Will any agency or agencies regulate your business?

■ Management Team

The Management section of the business plan has its own component in every BizPlanBuilder master template except for the Service Business plan. The management team provides the leadership for your business and must include combined strength in both management and technical areas. The management team should be selected in such a manner that talents are complementary rather than overlapping or duplicated. You must ensure that all the key areas necessary to accomplish the goals and objectives of the company are within the strengths and talents of your management team.

Early on in your business, you will want people who are capable of handling multiple functions. As your company grows, your requirements will call for more specialization within the management team. A combination of experience, technical skills and energy will serve your company well. Recommended reading on this topic: *The Greatest Management Principle in the World*, by Michael LeBoeuf, Ph.D.

In addition to the management team, this template may also include relevant sections for a board of directors, staffing, strategic help, and related human resources.

■ Boards of Directors and Advisors

▶ **Do It in BizPlanBuilder**

The BizPlanBuilder Masters also has a template letter for inviting professionals to be on a board of advisors.

The Board of Directors is usually vested financially in the company and in a large company may take the form of venture capitalists. They may also bring specific business experience to the management team. Directors vote to approve acquisitions, financing, officers' compensation and other key decisions.

An entity that sounds similar in purpose is the Board of Advisors. The difference between an advisor and a director is that a director usually has a fiduciary and therefore legal responsibility to shareholders. Advisors offer advice on matters often concerning marketing, product development, planning and organizing, and the like in return for stock in the company or other compensation or benefits.

The BizPlanBuilder Manage Your Business Masters includes a template letter [Invite to Board of Directors] for inviting prospective members to your board. Such individuals can be recipients of your business plan or summaries thereof.

■ Staffing

Understanding the strengths and weaknesses of your staffing is important to the investor. Although you may not have all your staff in place when you begin, a plan of action that addresses how and when you will fill the gaps is required. A new business may turn to consultants and other professionals for specific areas of expertise. Both small and large companies should seek the professional services of an attorney and an accountant during business startup—the latter is particularly important in preparing the financials that are discussed more fully in Part 4, Completing the Financial Plan.

■ Strategic Alliances

Strategic alliances can strengthen and broaden your potential market as well as add talent to your management team. Some of the alliances you may seek include. Though not included in BizPlanBuilder's Company Overview templates, this part of the business plan can also be used to describe any strategic alliances or partnerships you have formed or whom you have researched and have, or will, approach. A strategic alliance is any joint initiative between one company and another that seeks to maximize the marketing opportunity for their mutual benefit. An example would be a Value Added Reseller (VAR) that bundles its computer hardware with another company's software.

Investors want to know if you have or plan to have such an advantage. The fact that you have researched such an opportunity and/or formed such a partnership will attract investment or the willingness of a bank to loan you the money to make your business a reality. For more information, refer to Part 5, Funding Resources for Your Plan.

■ Company Overview for the Service/Bank Loan Plan

Unlike the business plans for larger and more complex operations, the Company Overview in the BizPlanBuilder Service/Bank Loan Master is a more versatile document in which a small company or sole proprietorship can describe the nature and advantage of its service. In this context, the Company Overview is an extension of the topics covered in the Executive Summary, which has sections in it that are analogous to the business structure narratives in the Company Overviews of the other BizPlanBuilder Master templates. The Company Overview for the Service/Bank Loan plan includes the following sections:

- **Company Mission.** This is similar to the Mission Statement described earlier.

- **Business Description.** A brief description of your business and the personal skills you will utilize.

- **Startup Costs.** The initial out-of-pocket expenses for covering the costs of such items as stationery, office equipment, and the like.

- **Customer Base.** Potential clients whose needs your business will meet.

- **Competition.** Anyone you expect will be offering the same services as yours and any advantages you have over them.

- **Business Challenges.** Such challenges as who can replace you in time of illness, and the like.

- **Pricing Structure.** The kind of pricing structure—e.g., single-pricing, corporate incentive, etc.—that will ensure a healthy cash flow.

- **Industry Trends.** How might change impact your business?

- **Technology.** This section chiefly deals with your e-business initiative.

- **Growth Factors.** A general statement about the economic health of the area in which you do business.

Despite the brevity of this component, some research will be required before you can answer each section.

■ Company Overview Checklist

√ Has your local government agency approved and registered the name of your company?

√ If your company's name is different from your own, have you filed a Fictitious Business Name statement?

√ Have you reviewed the different forms of business and determined which is appropriate for your company?

√ Have you established a management team that provides leadership for your business in both management and technical areas?

√ Do the strengths and talents of your management team match the goals and objectives of your company?

√ Does your Board of Directors bring specific business experience to the management team?

√ If your staffing is not complete, do you have an established action plan to share with your prospective investors?

√ Have you considered strategic alliances to help strengthen and broaden your potential market or to add talent to your management team?

■ BizPlanBuildercise 3.3(A): Review the Company Overview Templates

In this exercise, compare sections of the Company Overview component in a Service/Bank Loan plan and the Company Overview from the Angel/VC business plan templates.

1. Launch BizPlanBuilder if necessary.

2. Choose to work on the LogaTorial example or your own business plan.

3. Double-click the **Company Overview** icon ⬢ Company Overview in the current plan area in the Item list—or **Overview** as its template icon may be labeled in other plans. (Click **OK** to close warning window if necessary.)

4. Maximize the Document pane as desired.

5. Review the template thoroughly by scrolling through the template document and reading its content, placeholders, and Expert Comments. Highlights of your review might include the following:

   ▫ **Service/Bank Loan plan.** Notice the emphasis on describing your company vis-à-vis your competition. Research is necessary for this part of your narrative, including such variables as comparative pricing structures as shown below.

Service	LogaTorial Prepress Service	[Competitor 1]	[Competitor 2]	[Competitor 3]
[Service 1]	[$XX-XX]	[$XX-XX]	[$XX-XX]	[$XX-XX]
[Service 2]	[$XX-XX]	[$XX-XX]	[$XX-XX]	[$XX-XX]
[Service 3]	$[$XX-XX]	[$XX-XX]	[$XX-XX]	[$XX-XX]

Competitive Pricing

The major strengths and weaknesses of our competitors include [example: price, location, quality].

The major competitors' objectives and strategies are [list].

The major competitors' most likely response to current [economic, social, culture, demographic, geographic, political, governmental, technological, and competitive] trends affecting our industry will be [list likely competitor responses].

□ **Retail, Angel/VC, and Internet Plan.** The Company Overview for these plans is concise. The key sections are legalistic in nature, such as the company's legal description and its government regulation dimension. Other templates correspond to what are just sections in the Service/Bank Loan plan Company Overview. For example, a template for describing the Competition exists in these larger business plans. A section describing Management is delegated to its own template, which can be reviewed in the following exercise.

■ BizPlanBuildercise 3.3(B): Review the Management Template

In this exercise you will review the Management template, which can be seen as a continuation of the Company Overview section. Even though the Service/Bank Loan plan does not include a Management template, a small business, sole proprietor, or even a freelancer should including this component in whole or in part. If you are going to manage yourself, consider adding a fuller description of your ability to do so and list and describe those individuals who are advising you, such as your accountant, attorney, consultant, or other kinds of mentors who show that you know where to find expertise, which is an expertise in itself.

> The Management template has a section for Outside Support. This section can be added to the plans for smaller and freelance business ventures.

Outside Support
Our outside management advisors provide tremendous support for management decisions and creativity.

[xxx]	Accountant / CPA
[xxx]	Corporate Attorney
[xxx]	[Type of] Consultant

❖ Provide résumés of outside support staff in the Supporting Documents.

❖ An organizational chart describing necessary business functions and relationships may also be included in Supporting Documents.

❖ Include each person's actual résumé in the Supporting Documents.

---

1. Double-click the Management icon [🛡 Management] in the BizPlanBuilder window's Item list. If you are working on a Service/Bank Loan plan, double-click the Management template from any of the other Master templates.

2. Click **OK** to close the BizPlanBuilder warning window.

3. Maximize the Document pane as desired.

4. Review the sections of this template.

5. Close BizPlanBuilder without saving.

■ Review Questions 3.3

1. If your business is a sole proprietorship, how is it taxed by the Federal government? What are the implications if you have a loss?

_____

_____

2. What is the difference between a general and a limited partnership?

_____

_____

_____

_____

3. What must a company do to incorporate?

_____

_____

_____

_____

4. Tom Herman is trying to decide whether his new metal plating company should be a C-Corporation or an S-Corporation. The shareholders are Tom and his three sons. He expects the company to have sales of about $500,000 per year with slow annual growth (5%) but to show annual losses of about $75,000 for the first three years due to startup costs. What do you suggest?

_____

_____

_____

_____

5. What is a Limited Liability Company? Why would a firm organize as an LLC?

_____

_____

_____

_____

6. Included in the company overview is a description of the government regulations that your business faces. What should you emphasize in this description?

_____

_____

_____

_____

_____

■ Activities 3.3

> **The activities below and for the rest of the course are freely adaptable to best suit the BizPlanBuilder Masters template that you use. You can also perform these activities as hypothetical—role-playing—exercises, using your own or the LogaTorial example. This strategy will make you familiar with the BizPlanBuilder interface and help you to customize your business plan.**

1. After reviewing the Company Overview component in BizPlanBuildercise 3.3, fill out the legal business description section of the document—or prepare notes for filling this document out later for this activity and for subsequent ones—making a decision about the legal form of your proposed business. Are you able to complete the Government Regulations section? How could you find out the details that you need to complete this section?

2. Using the section of the Management component that discusses the management team, what are the key positions for your company? What type of credentials should these people have?

3. Using the section of the Management component that discusses staffing, what additional staff will be needed in your first year? What outside support personnel will you need?

Some men see things as they are and ask, "Why?"
I dream things that never were and ask, "Why not?"
—*George Bernard Shaw*

Service /Product Strategy

This section is about the crucial place that the company's services or products have in the business plan. Even if your service or product in some prototype or beta testing phase, you will want to describe what the finished service or product will be in detail.

You can talk about it a number of ways, "from concept to cash," "from patent to product," "from A to Z," "from soup to nuts," "the whole 9 yards." Determining your future products, projected development, and how you will produce and deliver to your customers are key aspects of Product Strategy. This provides the real bloodline for your business.

In BizPlanBuilder, the Angel/VC and Internet masters provide a Product Strategy template. The Retail master does, too; however it is specifically designed for the sale and distribution of a product in which indirect manufacturer and distributor relationships must be described in a narrative format. The Product Strategy template of the other two plans is designed for the manufacture of a product or the provision of a service—so it can be edited to serve as a service strategy narrative.

From this point on, you should think of products and services interchangeably in this section. A service such as a restaurant is provides a service product: food served at a table or as carryout. And a product such as an iPod provides and facilitates a product service: portable, downloadable music and podcasting. The list is endless.

■ Current Service/Product

The current service or product description in your business plan should highlight its unique, distinct, or improved features and benefits. Many companies begin with a unique idea for a product or service that grows in scope over time. These product insights, and subsequent methods of exploiting them, often provide a compelling story. This section is of special interest to bankers or investors. They will want to know what sets your product or service apart from the competition, how well you produce your product, and what new trails your company may be blazing.

▶ **Do It in BizPlanBuilder**

The Manage Your Business Masters has instructions and a template for creating a trademark application.

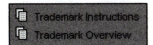

Proprietary Technology

Proprietary technology is a new or unique product, application, or base of knowledge (sometimes called intellectual property) in the market that may be protected under patents, copyrights, trademarks, and the like. Your company gains this legal protection when registering with the U.S. Department of Commerce's Patent or Trademark Offices. The registration of your product provides you with legal protection and recourse in a court of law if a competitor tries to copy your idea.

A large portion of a company's worth is often in patents, copyrights and trademarks. If your company deals in these areas, it is important to keep your legal status current and to maintain a thorough inventory of your intellectual property.

A good resource to consult for information about patents, copyrights, and trademarks is the Patent Café Web site at **http://www.patentcafe.com**. Your BizPlanBuilder Managing Your Business Masters also supplies documents for managing trademarks.

Useful Features/Benefits

Customer satisfaction is increased if she or he understands the features and benefits of your product. Features and benefits must address the customer's needs and wants and must distinguish your product from the competition.

The product should be designed with the customer's needs in mind. How well and how cost effectively these features actually produce desired benefits and results to your customers will determine whether your product (and company) experiences boom or bust.

A service, too, should address unmet needs or find a niche in a preexisting service sector that has not been fully exploited or has not experienced an infusion of competition. It needs to be a "package" and a price that no one else offers.

■ Research and Development (R&D)

All companies need ongoing product and service development. (Retail and Internet entrepreneurs should also keep up to date on advances made in the line of products or services they sell.) Your target market, competitors, and current technologies are always changing. To maintain a competitive edge, you must keep on top of new developments that will affect your business. Some of the questions to consider are:

- Do you have a plan for a new product or new technology?

- Have you established milestones to track your development?

- Have you listed your accomplishments (example: prototype, development, lab testing, and the like)?

- Have you determined all the true costs of your product development efforts and are these costs for research, testing and development, and so forth in line with your budget?

- What are your competitors spending on R&D?

- Have you thought of a joint developer, supplier—domestic or outsource?

Both small and large companies need to allocate resources to R&D. This may range from staffing a complete department to research customer needs and develop new products to simply keeping abreast of industry changes through publications and conferences.

In the Manage Your Business Masters, there are templates for such R&D issues as a Product Test Agreement [Product Feedback Survey] for beta testers—and a customer satisfaction questionnaire [Service Feedback Survey] suitable for service-oriented ventures.

Product Selection/Development Criteria

As your company grows, selecting your new products or services becomes a bigger gamble. When you had an idea, you put it together and then tested it to see if it sold. With the marketplace becoming more demanding, competition becoming fiercer, and development and marketing costs soaring, present and future product cycle times generally require more thorough evaluation before selecting new items to develop.

More ideas and concepts are being created now than ever before. If your company has put together its vision, mission, goals and objectives (as discussed in the Vision and Mission section previously), you will have a big head start on the product selection process. With these planning tools in place, certain concepts will fit more readily than others, and your company focus will be easier to maintain.

Writing a Product Selection Criteria—an example is found in the Angel/VC Product Strategy template—for your company may prove to be one of your wisest investments of time and effort for your management group. First of all, it can pay off in wisely selected, profit-rich products or services for development. It can also save your company both financial losses and considerable grief by facilitating the wise discarding of losing product concepts that may burden your company.

The factors that should be covered in your selection criteria include financial benefit to company, relatively low investment requirements, positive return on investment (ROI), fit with present strategy, feasibility to develop and produce, relatively low risk and the time required to see intended results.

Your finished Product Selection Criteria may be very short and to the point. Or it may cover a wide range of product questions as they relate to the various departments in your company. By including A Product Selection Criteria in your business plan, you show the world that you recognize what your company can produce and that you understand that product focus and execution will carry your company to the profit levels that are envisioned.

Planned Products

After you have presented your current products and how your company decides on its new products, it's time to give a preview of your upcoming hits. Your product intentions and projections should be described in the same detail as your current product or service offerings. After all, the target reader of your business plan is usually more interested in what you foresee than what you have done. This is where the target reader can assist your company's efforts in some way—ideas, investment, management assistance, or materials.

Not only do you want to lay out your product plans in this section, but you also want to show how you will achieve them. Investors are exposed to dozens or hundreds of ideas each year. Most often they are unimpressed until they see a good idea with an excellent plan of execution. In your business plan, show the reader both your planned product concepts and how the products will be completed and delivered.

For a small, service-oriented company, this can be expressed as the entire Product Strategy section:

Product Strategy

Sun & Fun Bike Touring has recently begun offering bike touring vacation packages throughout Northern California, Mexico and Wyoming.

Our principal service consists of 6-day bike tour vacation packages for people who enjoy an active and adventurous vacation.

The first bike touring trip, Sun & Fun in Baja California, was introduced in late 1993. Since then, we have also developed new biking tours for 2006 in the following five areas: Monterey, Redwood Country (Humboldt County), Napa Valley Wine Country, and Yosemite in California and Yellowstone in Wyoming.

In response to demonstrated needs of our market, in October 2006 we will begin to include weekend getaways for families, tandem-bike touring and custom tours. New 6-day bike tours are now being developed for many areas, including the Snake River area of Idaho, the San Juan Islands of British Columbia, Alaska, France and Spain. These tours will begin in April 2007.

■ Production and Delivery

This section discusses any proposed site location, costs of your product, facilities and logistics. The emphasis must be on the productive use of capital, labor, material resources, manufacturing processes, vendor relations, experience, and distribution requirements. Statements are needed that indicate initial volume and expansion requirements, as well as product/process complexity, uniqueness, and costs.

Production

At this stage you need to explain how you are going to make your future product or deliver your future services. Determining your equipment, material and labor requirements, as well as their price and availability, can be critical factors in the production process. Other considerations include alternate sources/materials, inventory requirements, and care and handling of hazardous materials.

You need to determine the full capacity of your present facility and how your new product plans will translate into manufacturing schedules. How will new product plans affect the way production is done now? Let the reader of your business plan know that you've done your homework and that your production capabilities will not be overrun by the proposed products selected for future development and production.

Costs

To determine the cost of your product, it is important to quantify your business costs in terms of production rates, capacity constraints, or required quality assurance and safety programs. Include quantity discounts, if applicable.

In evaluating the cost of the same product from other companies, you should determine why and how your costs are more competitive. This information will be important to the banker or investor who is looking at the return on investment. If subcontract or assembly work is required, list parts, vendors, lead time, costs, and so on. Include information on how the future product cost will rise.

Facilities

The manufacturing facility provides needed space for initial production and expansion to meet projected demand. Site selection includes the following considerations:

- Room and cost for expansion

- Land and construction costs

- Transportation cost and route access for common carrier

- Risks and insurance

- Packaging and material costs and availability

- Labor pool availability, skills, costs

- Local ordinances, licensing and permit requirements

- Government assistance (roads, training, exemptions, etc.)

- Government restrictions and requirements (OSHA, NLRB, etc.)

- Community attitudes toward business and manufacturing

- Continued operating costs (utilities, communications, etc.)

Packaging and Transportation

The primary function of a product package is the protection and safety of the product. The package must be designed to protect the product during transportation over a specific period of time in varying climates. Finally, a package can be an effective marketing tool by differentiating your product from that of your competition. Both the packaging and the transportation of your product convey an image to the customer and must be balanced with the cost, availability and competitive products on the market.

Product Fulfillment

Product fulfillment is an important part of customer satisfaction. In the case of a service product, this might mean how quickly the service is provided and how quickly it is completed.

Providing a channel to monitor and manage the delivery, billing, warranty, and repair of your products will ensure customer satisfaction and repeat sales. Some or all of these services can be supplied directly by your company. Increasing numbers of businesses are contracting some of these services to companies specializing in these areas.

■ Product/Service Strategy Checklist

√ Is your product registered with the U.S. Department of Commerce's Patent or Trademark Offices?

√ Do the features and benefits of your product or service address your customer's needs and wants?

√ Does your business plan describe how your company will react to competition, change in market, and the like?

√ Does your company have resources allocated to Research and Development?

√ Are you referring to your company's stated vision, mission, goals, and objectives when selecting new products or proposing a new service?

√ Are you researching how your product can be regularly improved in order to maintain its competitive position, market value, and price point?

√ Can you communicate both your planned concepts and how the products will be completed and delivered in your business plan?

√ Do you know how your product or service will be produced and delivered?

√ Do you know the cost of your product or service?

√ Have you considered all of the site selection factors when considering the location of your product's production facility?

√ What type of packaging does your product need?

√ How can your customers reach you if they have comments or problems with your product or service?

√ How will your product be shipped or delivered? Or, what kind of service mix will you deliver? (If you market software, you may choose to "ship" products only as downloads. If your service is a sushi restaurant, will you deliver?)

√ If you are planning a retail or Internet business:

  □ Who will be your manufacturer/distributor?

  □ What will be the number of product turns?

  □ What kind of pricing arrangements will allow for healthy initial margins?

■ BizPlanBuildercise 3.4: Review Product Strategy Template

In this exercise you will review the Product Strategy tempate in the Angel/VC master.

1. Launch BizPlanBuilder if necessary.

2. Choose to work on the LogaTorial example or your own business plan.

3. Expand the ▣ BizPlanBuilder Masters library in the Item list by clicking the plus sign.

   a. Expand the ▣ Angel/VC Plan library.

   b. Right-click on Product Strategy and click **Open**.

   c. In the for-viewing-only message window, click **OK**

   OR

   If your plan already includes a Product Strategy template, double-click the Product Strategy in the current plan part of the Item list and close the message window.

4. Maximize the Document pane as desired.

5. Review the component thoroughly by scrolling through the template document and reading its content, placeholders, and Expert Comments.

> The Product Strategy template of the Angel/VC template contains useful telephone numbers and a hyperlink to the U.S. Patent Office's Web site.

Proprietary Technology / Intellectual Property

❖ Most Venture Capitalists (many angel investors too) are nuts about IP (Intellectual Property) protection, leveraging IP assets, etc. "What is your IP Strategy?" What do you have that you can protect so well that an 800 pound gorilla can't come in and re-engineer everything in 6 months or less and then pound you in the market.

❖ If you have a ton of IP, but none of it is truly 'unique'. It is more a compilation of many things from many sources. While that has value, the question is, How Much and at What Cost?

Our products are protected under the following:

❖ List any patents, copyrights, trademarks, licenses your company owns.

❖ For patent and trademark information, go to www.pto.gov

❖ General Patent and Trademark Information: [703] 557-INFO.

❖ Status Information for a Particular Trademark: [703] 557-5249.

Powered x BizPlanBuilder®   1

6. If desired, close BizPlanBuilder.

■ Review Questions 3.4

1. What is "proprietary technology?" Why register it?

_____

_____

_____

2. The product life cycle is a popular theory that explains the birth and death of many products. Which stage do you think will provide the greatest opportunities for profit and success? Which stage contains the greatest risk?

_____

_____

_____

_____

_____

_____

3. Where in BizPlanBuilder would you look for product or service development resources? List the ones that you find.

_____

_____

_____

_____

_____

4. The Pet Accessory Manufacturing Company supplies pet toys, treats and grooming products to a wide variety of wholesalers and retailers across the country. They are setting up a formal Product Selection Criteria to analyze new product ideas. What selection criteria would you suggest as guidelines?

_____

_____

_____

_____

_____

5. The Pet Accessory Manufacturing Company is projecting rapid growth and planning a new manufacturing facility. What should be some key site selection criteria for the new facility?

_____

_____

_____

_____

_____

_____

6. What is product fulfillment for a service provider such as a brew pub?

_____

_____

_____

_____

_____

_____

■ Activities 3.4

1. In BizPlanBuildercise 3.4, use the Product Strategy component to describe your product (or service), its features, and history. Try to fill out the Current Product section—or the section that applies to your business—with real or trial information.

2. Look at the product or service from your customers' point of view. After you have filled out the relevant section, determine the single most important advantage or benefit that your product brings to your customers. In the Product Plan, these are the Customer Return on Investment and Useful Features/Benefits sections.

3. Does your company have a plan for its research and development strategy? Fill out or take notes for the Research and Development section of the Product Strategy component in BizPlanBuildercise 3.4. Why would a form such as this impress potential investors? (If you are using the Retail master, analyze your relationships with manufacturers and distributors.)

He who excels at resolving difficulties does so before they arise.
He who excels in conquering his enemies triumphs
before threats materialize.
— Sun Tzu, The Art of War

Market Analysis

The marketing templates in BizPlanBuilder's masters are that part of the business plan narrative in which you describe the existing and projected marketplace in which you intend to introduce and promote your company as well as your produces and services. There are two parts of your business plan narrative that discuss marketing. The Market Analysis section presents your understanding of the market, your customers, your competition, and has solid information to back those assessments. The Marketing Plan or Strategy shows how you intend to use the marketing analysis to position your product or service and realize the sales figures that you project. That is, through price, positioning, sales techniques and channels (which now includes everything from showrooms to telephone banks to spam), and advertising. You can read more about the market plan's narrative in the BizPlanBuilder handbook that shipped with your software.

> **The order in which these marketing sections appear is up to you—but obviously, whichever *markets* your plan best should go first.**

These templates also provide a venue for discussing the behavior or individual habits of the consumer you intend to target, from a certain demographic to other companies if your venture is business-to-business, and how you intend to persuade them to use your service or buy your product. No matter what type of business you are in, the final decision to buy or not buy is made by a consumer.

The better you understand this decision-making process, the better you can sway that decision. This part of the business plan is also where you are *marketing* it potential investors or a bank loan officer. You convince them to buy your idea by how much marketing analysis you do to justify that idea. As in the previous section, the term *product* means *service*, too, throughout this discussion.

In addition to the Market Analysis template, BizPlanBuilder provides other marketing templates that can further detail the marketing scope of your business plan. These include the Market Opportunity and Market Strategy templates provided in certain masters. The Service/Bank Loan Plan features a Market Strategy/Marketing Plan template—and its Company Overview template contains many of the same business plan narrative sections covered here.

■ Market Definition

The following discussion is based on the Market Analysis template used in the Angel/VC, Internet, and Retail masters Each plan's template differs, however they are all the same in design and intent—this is where your business plan describes what is known about your target market. Several key components of this analysis include an industry analysis, a market segment analysis, an analysis of your competitors' strengths and weaknesses and discovery of unexploited opportunities.

Industry Analysis

An industry analysis begins with collecting information on the size, growth and structure of the industry as well as target market coverage, marketing objectives, marketing mix, and tactics. This information is used to monitor changes and exploit weaknesses in the marketplace that give your company a competitive edge. Some form of this same procedure also applies to retail ventures—whether it is a brick-and-mortar or an Internet-only business—and to sole proprietors working in a crowded field such as Molly LeDier's prepress services company, LogaTorial.

Market Segment

Within the industry, the market segment defines the market further by product/service feature, lifestyle of target consumers, season, and the like. Sources such as industry analyses, census reports, and trade journal studies help you define your market. To become the market leader in your product or service, your company must capture the biggest portion of sales in its market segment.

S.W.O.T. Analysis

The Product Plan contains a section for S.W.O.T.—Strengths, Weaknesses, Opportunities, and Threats—analysis.

> **The S.W.O.T. analysis below is written for a generic product and requires some quick editing to address your specific product or service.**

Strengths, Weaknesses, Opportunities & Threats (SWOT Analysis)

Strengths

❖   In covering your strengths, be sure to place at least as much (if not more) emphasis on marketing (as well as your management team) as on your product.

LogaTorial Prepress Service brings a considerable pool of product and marketing strengths to the [market name] marketplace. In terms of product strength, [product name] has several distinct advantages over the competition. First is its marked advancement in [xxx technology / operating efficiency / customer options / functionality].

❖   Address these areas for each of your products. How else is the product favorably differentiated from the competition:

❖   In delivery?

❖   In actual performance?

❖   In quality and reliability?

❖   In production efficiencies?

❖   In breadth of line and / or options and enhancements?

LogaTorial Prepress Service's greatest strength is the innovative approach it has taken to designing and building [product names]s. Being a smaller company, LogaTorial Prepress Service has greater flexibility than its larger competitors to try different materials and methods since it does not have to consult with an entire panel of engineers or obtain unanimous approval from multiple divisions to implement a viable new customer-approved solution. This means that the latest breakthroughs in design will be implemented and tested here before comparable products are even off the drawing board at competitive companies.

In marketing, our most powerful assets are [x].

❖   Describe your strengths:

Strengths and Weaknesses

In identifying the strengths and weaknesses of your competitor's product or service, you are evaluating the competitor's coverage of the market and its success in meeting customer demand. By exploiting this weakness, you can improve both your service or product and your position in the market and convey that you are (or will be) strong where your competitors are weak.

Unexploited Opportunities

Based on your marketing analysis, you may discover additional niches and opportunities to explore. Often a successful product or service can be leveraged through new distribution channels, licensing, packaging, and so on. Identifying your top market opportunities will help you focus your marketing efforts.

Threats

Are the same as environmental risks and are discussed in later in this section. In the Market Analysis, you can assess those risks there or describe them in more detail in the Risk template available in most plan masters.

■ Customer Profile

Knowing exactly who you're selling to is crucial to obtaining favorable response from your investors. The customer profile may include consumer adoption, economic factors, demographics, psychographics, and influencers.

Consumer Adoption Process

The consumer adoption process is based on the idea that certain kinds of people will accept and use your product in different stages. These classes of adoption in the order of greatest willingness to try your product are: innovators, early adopters, early majority, late majority, and laggards. Each group generally has different traits that separate it from the others, such as age, race, family stage, income or geographic location. The groups also tend to read or listen to specific media and prefer different types of sales information.

Economic Factors

Economic factors are those that affect how people spend their money. The more money an individual has in savings, the more income available for leisure items such as travel, entertainment and sporting goods, and the greater potential to purchase higher-priced durable products such as cars, appliances, and housing. Issues for consumers include level of personal debt, income expectations, taxes, interest rates, and savings.

Demographics

Demographics are based on research by the national census, local governmental agencies, and private firms. Demographic data is also being collected from the Web-browsing public and online shoppers, which is, by happenstance, making it easier to pinpoint a target market. These studies list such items as average income, average age, average family size and a variety of other information about consumers who live in a given geographic area. They can also provide much information about individual consumer habits, too. Nevertheless, excellent—and traditional—sources for demographic studies can still be had from your local Chamber of Commerce, your state's Department of Commerce, and the local library. Much information can be found online, too, at no cost, from Census Bureau (www.census.gov) and other state and federal government Internet sources.

As a business owner, you must develop a "profile" of your primary customer or customers. These will be the people you believe have demand for your product or service and will be making the purchase decision. For example, if you are trying to target an upscale audience, say the readers of *Smithsonian Magazine* and similar publications, you will need information about their "average" subscriber. *Smithsonian Magazine,* for example, to lure advertisers, publishes an online media kit that provides much of the kind of information you will need.

This online media kit is published by *Smithsonian Magazine* to attract advertisers—but such free data can be "repurposed" to fit your business plan's consumer target.

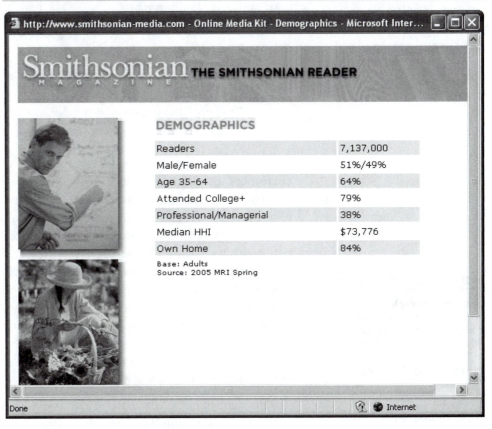

Although this "average" subscriber is not characteristic of all *Smithsonian Magazine* readers, you are closer to having a customer profile on which to base your product line selection (depth and breadth), pricing objectives, promotional message, media channels, and location selection. Other magazines, radio and television stations, and other kinds of media vendors also make such information available that would normally cost you a lot of money to compile yourself.

Influencers

Another consideration in profiling your customer is to understand who influences purchase decisions. These are the people who:

- Initiate the inquiry for your service or product

- Influence the decision(s) to buy

- Decide which product or service to buy

- Permit the purchase to be made

Sometimes the decision maker and the one who approves the purchase of products and services is the same person. It is the Chief Financial Officer (CFO), however, who signs the paperwork after other managers have submitted their recommendations.

Your presentation and proposal must show that you grasp this relationship. If you don't, an imperfect understanding can make or break a critical part of your business plan narrative.

■ Competition

Two hikers were in the woods when suddenly a bear appeared.
One quickly took off his pack, pulled out his sneakers and put them on.
"You don't think you can outrun that bear do you?" asked his companion.
"No," he replied, "I just need to outrun you!"

It is important that you are aware of the many competitors perceived by your customers (consciously or otherwise). Competition not only comes from companies in the same industry, but also from other sources interested in your customers' money. For example: a swimming pool service contractor not only competes with other swimming pool service contractors, he competes with a customer's interest in having a manicured and weed-free lawn, the health club and its indoor pool, the golf club, and other providers ranging from other residential upkeep services to a host of leisure-time and recreational activity providers—and don't forget the local water park. If you acknowledge these competitors—and develop marketing strategies to propel your service or product not only ahead of others in your industry, but to the top of your customer's priority list—you will impress investors and take a commanding lead in your business.

BizPlanBuilder's Marketing Analysis component contains a subsection for analyzing competition. However, for more complex business plans, you may need to include a separate assessment of competition using the Competition templates available in the Retail, Angel/VC, and Internet masters.

Evaluating Competition

It is important to know as much about your competitors' businesses as you do your own business. Here are some areas you should know about your competitors' product in comparison to your own.

▶ Do It in BizPlanBuilder

Learn how to exploit the Web for information about competition. Click the Biz-Plan Workshop button on

the toolbar and then

click ■ Business Plan Workshop .

In the Business Plan Workshop's table of contents pane, click the **Competition** link under **Market Analysis.**

Products and Services

How do your competitors' products or services compare against your own, using the same criteria you used when evaluating your own product: color, size, price, and on—or services: levels of coverage, rates, quality, guarantees, and the like?

Organization

What are your competitors' organizations like? Can they make fast and accurate decisions? Will they respond quickly to changes you make? Are their management and staff competent? Are they leaders or followers in the market? How are they funded? Do you consider them to be viable competitors in the future?

Track Record

Customers will often choose a contractor or supplier because of its track record. How does your record compare to that of your competitors? Are they well known in the industry? An assessment of your stability compared to that of your competitors can be a real selling point to your customer, especially if you're selling a product that will require future servicing—or a service that requires routine visits, upgrading, and the like.

■ Risk

*Every noble acquisition is attended with its risk;
he who fears to encounter the one
must not expect to obtain the other.*
— *Pietro Metastasio*

Any discussion of the business environment must include the various kinds of risks. In researching risk, it is important to remember that it is impossible to anticipate all possible risks and alleviate them. The best you can do is to identify as many of them as possible and anticipate solutions to handle them before they occur. The best strategy to alleviate risk is to diversify. Use multiple suppliers, sell multiple products, attempt to keep up with new technologies and purchase insurance for those risks you can insure against, such as fire, theft, and illness.

Risk can be broken down into two major categories: business and environmental. BizPlanBuilder offers a specialized Risk component for all plans—except the more basic Service/Bank Loan plan—to describe the potential threats to your new venture.

Business Risk

Each industry has its own set of unique business risks. For example, some industries have high capital needs, others have a seasonal business cycle, and still others depend on a limited group of customers and suppliers.

Cost Structure

The first and perhaps the largest risk is the cost structure of the industry. This is directly related to the amount of fixed assets or capital required to operate your business. As discussed earlier, the amount of capital required is determined by the type of business you want to start and the structure of the market. In general, the more capital your industry or business requires, the larger your fixed expenses will be. If you wanted to revive the Tucker Torpedo[*] and compete with BMW or DaimlerChrysler, you would need tens of millions of dollars to open your business. You would need to purchase or build a factory and buy an expensive amount of equipment to produce automobiles—not to mention car designers, advertising, distribution, and all the other variables. You would have debt and rent payments that would be fixed whether you produced 100,000 cars or you produced a handful of cars. The dollars you would lose each month when not producing and selling your break-even volume of cars could rapidly force you out of business.

Competition and Industry Growth

Competition from the national brands or from present or new regionally based companies poses a risk to your company. If the market for your product continues to grow, the major national companies will likely devote greater resources to this segment. Developing a niche in the market, competitive pricing and customer service will minimize this risk. In the service and retail sector, the competition can, of course, be localized and even on the same block if you run a grass-cutting business or sell fresh hot bagels.

Product Liability

Product liability insurance is a necessary evil in today's business environment.

A large damage award against a company not adequately covered by insurance could adversely affect its financial position.

Profit Margin

Profit margin (the percentage of net profits to sales) versus the volume of sales is another type of risk. A good example of this risk would be to compare a grocery store to a jewelry store.

The grocery store sells its entire inventory every other day; however, net profit margin is only one percent. The business makes its money through high sales volume. The grocery store owner can determine changes in customer demand quickly and adjust for those changes within a few days. The jeweler, on the other hand, holds a piece of jewelry on average 90 days before she sells it. Because of the amount of profit she makes on each individual item, she only has to sell a few large items to equal the profit of the grocery store. However, risk lies in the jeweler's inability to detect changes in demand quickly and to adjust her marketing strategies for these changes quickly. The grocery owner can see a slowing in business within two days and adjust for it immediately. The jeweler will need

---

[*] The "car of the future" designed and built by Preston Tucker in the 1940s, whose story, immortalized in the film *Tucker* (1988), is as much fascinating for what it teaches about innovative methods he used to start and capitalize his dream.

90 days to make those same adjustments. The only way to minimize the profit-volume risk for the jeweler is to have surplus cash to support operations until she can adjust her buying habits.

Seasonal Business

Is your business a seasonal one or are your sales steady throughout the year? If your business is highly seasonal, you risk having to estimate your inventory and cash needs as the season begins, matures and closes. Typically, in the retail clothing business, you need to order your fall inventory in June, your winter inventory in September and so on. Your risk is twofold. You face the possibility of buying too much inventory and not being able to sell it or of buying too little inventory and selling out early. The second part of the risk is that customer attitudes change, and the styles you ordered may not be popular.

Complementary Industries

You also need to understand how your business depends on complementary industries. If you were a plumbing contractor or a hardware store owner, your business would prosper or starve depending on how the housing industry performs. When new homes are in demand, the housing industry grows and your business has the opportunity to succeed. However, as interest rates go up, tax laws change and new home demand declines, you face declining sales over which you have no control. The best way to lessen your dependence on any one industry is to expand (diversify) your business.

Substitution

Vulnerability to substitution is a risk that your business might face. You need to see your industry in the broadest possible way. By doing so, you should be able to foresee changes. Instead of being hurt, you can take advantage of them to further expand your business.

Suppliers

If you depend on any one or just a few suppliers, they can control your business. If they raise their prices, you can be trapped into paying those increased prices. In a low inflationary economy, you might not be able to pass those price increases on to your customers. If your supplier decreases his trade terms from 60 days to 30 days, your cash flow will be hurt without your having any control. Finally, if your supplier has only a limited inventory, his ability to meet your demands might be restricted. The best way to minimize supplier risk is to spread your purchases over a number of suppliers. The more you depend on a single supplier, the more risk your business faces.

Customers

Some of the same risks associated with a limited number of suppliers can apply to your customers as well. A good example is the lawn mower manufacturer whose only customer is a major retail chain. As the manufacturer faces rising costs of production, he attempts to pass those costs along to his customer. However, because the retail chain knows that it is responsible for 100% of the manufacturer's sales, the chain can refuse to pay the increased prices. The manufacturer is faced with no sales or sales at the old price and greatly reduced profits. The best strategy is to have as many credit-worthy customers as possible. Although it is advantageous to have guaranteed sales and know you will be paid for them, it is not a favorable trade-off to lose control of your pricing to your customer.

Personnel and Management

Success of the company is dependent upon its ability to attract and retain qualified personnel. Certainly in the initial stage, success also depends on the continued service of the founder and President, as well as other key executives. While continued employment of these individuals cannot be guaranteed, various incentives (including contracts) can be used to encourage their continued participation and minimize the risk of their departure.

Environmental Risk

Your business will also face risks that are not limited to the industry you operate in. An economical downturn or revised tax laws are examples of environmental risks that can affect a wide range of companies. The "real" environment, too, can factor in, especially if you want to get into the landscaping business (drought) or market winter sports equipment (a region-wide lack of snow due to the effects of global warming).

Economic

Adverse changes in prevailing economic conditions can have a negative impact on the company's projected business. In a recession, consumers decrease their expenditures and retailers are less inclined to make capital investments.

Economic risks such as inflation, recession, and rising interest rates affect the bottom line. You cannot alter these risks, but you can decrease the effects they will have on your company by understanding the impact of each. Perhaps the best strategy is diversification, offering numerous products or services to multiple market segments.

Weather

The weather can be a substantial risk to your business. You need to assess how changes in climate such as temperature and rainfall will affect your business. Included in this category is the potential for catastrophes such as hurricanes and tornados, fire, flood, drought, and the like. The best ways to avert these risks are good planning, good management and proper business insurance coverage.

Legal and Government

Almost without warning, a local ordinance can invalidate your business license, restrict your business operations by zoning laws or condemn your property in the public interest. (A recent Supreme Court ruling has renewed the debate over public domain and public benefit). Adult entertainment businesses, bars, brewpubs, and restaurants that permit smoking are particularly susceptible to change due to trends in antismoking legislation.

As with the legal risk, the business may be dependent on government regulations or contracts that affect your product or service. Staying abreast of legal issues facing your industry through industry publications will warn you of any significant changes.

■ Market Analysis Checklist

√ Have you conducted an industry analysis?

√ Have you conducted an analysis of the market within your industry?

√ Have you identified the strengths and weaknesses of your competitor's product or service?

√ Have you determined how you can turn your competitor's weaknesses into your company's strengths?

√ Have you developed a customer profile?

√ Have you analyzed your competitor's business and product?

√ Have you researched the business risks to your company?

- The cost structure of your industry
- Competition and industry growth
- Product and service liability
- Profit margin
- Dependence on complementary industries
- Vulnerability to substitution
- Limited number of suppliers
- Limited customer base
- Personnel and management issues

√ Have you researched the environmental risks?

- Economic conditions
- Weather
- Legal and governmental regulations

1. business plan.

▶ **Do It in BizPlanBuilder**

Clicking the More Tools button on the toolbar accesses the JIAN website, where you may want to investigate Marketing Builder, a full-featured marketing program that can be used before and after you establish your business. To do so, click the Business Marketing link under **Marketing Planning & Public Relations**.

■ BizPlanBuildercise 3.5: Review Marketing Analysis Template

In this exercise, open and review the Market template of your business plan. If you are using the Service/Bank Loan master, add a Market Analysis template to your current plan performing the appropriate steps.

1. Launch BizPlanBuilder if necessary.

2. Select the LogaTorial example or your own business plan.

3. Double-click | Market Analysis | in the current plan area of the Item list. (Click **OK** to close the warning window if necessary).

4. Maximize the Document pane as desired.

5. Review the component thoroughly by scrolling through the template document and reading its content, placeholders, and Expert Comments.

6. If desired, close BizPlanBuilder when you are done.

Optional Exercise. Review the Competition and Risk components of your business plan. Users of the Service/Bank Loan master should review the marketing analysis-oriented sections of their Company Overview template (Competition, Pricing Structure, Risk, etc.).

■ Review Questions 3.5

1. Why would a prospective lender want an industry analysis in your business plan?

_____

_____

_____

2. Your firm has developed a revolutionary new coffee vendor. It delivers coffee bar taste and everything from grande-style cup to a double espresso. Which category of consumer in the adoption process will your firm pursue? What promotion method will you use?

_____

_____

_____

3. What are demographics? Why is this information important?

_____

_____

_____

_____

4. Taking a broad view of competition, who or what would be the competition for a new 20-screen movie theater being built in your neighborhood?

_____

_____

5. Assume you are a toy manufacturer, supplying several lines of games, pre-school toys, dolls and action figures to Toys 'R Us, Target, and Wal-Mart. What specific business risks might you face?

_____

_____

_____

_____

6. Assume you operate a silk-screen t-shirt company that uses plastic inks and solvents to clean your equipment. What environmental risks do you face?

_____

_____

_____

_____

■ Activities 3.5

If you are using the Service/Bank Loan master, perform the following activities using the Market Strategy/Plan template. You can add templates or just sections of templates from other business plan masters to make your edits. For example, you can copy and paste a S.W.O.T. analysis section from the Angel/VC master to add its narrative to your service business plan.

1. Review and prepare notes that you might use to fill out the S.W.O.T. Analysis section of a Market Analysis template.

2. Who is your customer for your product or service? Using the Customers section of the applicable marketing component of your plan, describe your typical customer. You may fill out the section or prepare notes to do so later.

3. What kind of competition will you encounter? Research and fill out—or prepare notes—for the Competition template of your business plan.

4. Looking squarely at potential business risks, fill out or prepare notes for the Risk template of your business plan.

Business has only two functions—marketing and innovation.
— Milan Kundera

Marketing Plans

After you have drafted a market analysis component for your business plan, you must now show investors how you intend to use what you learned about your venture vis-à-vis target customers, competition, risks, and so on. This section takes that understanding and massages it a narrative about an overall market strategy: the Marketing Plan. Your market strategy is how you intend to sell your service or product to customers and clients. In its narrative form, it will need to sell to the potential investor or banker.

Strategy can be defined as the science of planning and directing large-scale operations, specifically of maneuvering forces into the most advantageous position prior to taking action. For that reason, it is important that this section of your business plan follow the definition of strategy because it will help you specifically define your marketing and sales activities, strengths, and direction. The Market Plan also strategizes how you will appropriately respond to business conditions and opportunities as they exist and change.

Your strategy needs to be logical and believable, well within your capabilities as a business and in line with your company direction and financial picture, as well as with your market need analysis. For example, you may have a great product idea. Perhaps you want to sell a slightly larger slice of American cheese so that it entirely covers a hamburger on a bun. You really would not have much of a chance to succeed unless you were a food conglomerate like Kraft, which is already dominant in the cheese business. Sooner rather than later, Kraft or another competitor could simply sell larger slices, too, and you would be out of business. No investor would believe in such a plan and, through honest analysis, neither would you. (Now, if you could patent putting a dill pickle slice inside a piece of American cheese and the product sells, you might be able to sell the idea and the company.)

■ Sales Strategy

▶ **Do It In BizPlanBuilder**

BizPlanBuilder features an Internet Strategy template in the all the plan masters except Service/Bank Loan.

🎁 Internet Strategy

This template can be used to elaborate how your business will tap the Internet as part of your marketing plan.

Positioning

All decisions are made by individuals, and all individuals are motivated by emotions. In the business environment, those emotions might be self-improvement, greed or the desire to impress others. Many of the same branding techniques used to convince consumers hold true for business customers as well. Positioning means how your customers perceive your company, product, or service relative to your competitors.

Pricing

As might be expected, price is one of the most effective marketing tools you use to promote your business. Price conveys image, affects demand and can help target your market segment. The Service/Bank Loan template, though designed for sole-proprietor business, even includes a Pricing Structure section in its comprehensive Company Overview component.

When considering what price to charge for your product or service, realize that price should not be based on production plus *some* profit. Instead, price should be based only on the value of your product or service to the customer! If that price does not generate the necessary profits, then changes must be made or the product line discontinued.

- How do we set prices? Is there a policy?

- Is the pricing competitive?

- Is there perceived value (it costs more, therefore it must be better) inherent in higher prices?

- Are prices based on costs—standard markup?

- Why are prices higher or lower than those of competitors?

- How elastic (the effect of pricing on demand for product) is the market for these products? How does consumer positioning affect elasticity?

- See also the Break-Even Analysis discussion in Part 4, Completing Your Financial Plan.

Pricing should follow directly from the company's overall goals and objectives as established by the owners. Every Market Plan will have its own related pricing strategy.

A wealthy and respected man once said that he looked around at what his competitors were charging and charged a little more. Don't be too quick to discount or go for the low-price leader position. Low-price leaders are incredibly efficient, massive marketers (Wal-Mart, Target, Home Depot). Many marketers like to emphasize the "offer" as the leading factor in sales response. Any salesperson can give away a product, and a competitor will surely displace your lowest price. Put yourself in your customer's position . . . relative to your price, isn't getting the job done far more important?

Pricing Strategies

One strategy is to "skim the cream" in the introduction phase by charging high prices when competition and substitution are minimal. Another strategy is to "match competition" by pricing slightly under competition to expand market share. A final strategy is to substantially underprice the market to exclude competitors. These strategies can be categorized into three areas: profit margin, sales, and status quo goals.

Profit-Oriented Goals

Profit-oriented goals include a specific net profit percentage or profit maximization. The first is a percentage goal and the second is a dollar value goal. The first goal might be to obtain a 10% net profit on sales and would bring in $10,000 on sales of $100,000. The second would attempt to earn $15,000, a higher profit, on sales of $200,000, which would be a 7.5% (lower) return.

Sales-Oriented Goals

Sales-oriented goals attempt to reach a specific dollar or unit sales growth objective, regardless of profit percentage or value. A sales-oriented goal might also be to obtain a specific market share. Typically, these goals are used to introduce a new product or a new market. Profit goals can be established later when the company has a consistent sales volume and customer base.

Status Quo Pricing

Status quo pricing is an effort to match the competition and not "rock the boat." This is usually the goal in a mature market where competition can be based on other competitive marketing features such as promotion, place, and packaging.

Discounts

When choosing a pricing strategy, in addition to the basic price of the product, you can offer discounts on single-order quantities, cumulative quantity orders, or on specific products. The owner might choose to use seasonal discounts to move more product during slow times of the year. Discounts can be used for either consumer goods or industrial products. Perhaps the best known discounts are the "frequent flier" discounts being offered by the airlines and, more recently, Detroit's allowing the general public to take advantage of its "employee discount programs" for the purchase of new automobiles.

Trade-in Allowances

Trade-in allowances are an effective way of lowering the final price to the customer without actually lowering the list price. Trade-in allowances are given for used goods when similar new products are purchased. They are standard in the automobile industry and in other industries that deal in industrial and durable goods.

Coupons

Coupons are another effective way of tailoring your pricing strategy for the consumer market. Coupons can be mailed directly to consumers' homes, delivered in local papers, or offered at the point of purchase and on the product itself. Many cost-conscious consumers shop only for those goods where they can use discount coupons. Coupons are an effective tool to reach various markets with the same product through pricing.

Internet sales have seen a new form of coupon cutting in which you type in a discount code to take advantage of additional discounts. The code can be delivered as e-mail, announced on a radio spot, or simply advertised directly on the checkout webpage.

Sales Terms and Credit

Included in pricing strategy are sales terms and credit. Sales terms allow customers to take a discount if the invoice is paid within a specified time period. A typical discount might be 2/10, net 30. This means the customer can take a two percent discount if the invoice is paid within 10 days, but the entire invoice is due within 30 days. Customers buying on credit create accounts receivable. The terms of these accounts can range from cash on delivery (C.O.D.) to due in 30, 45, 60, or 90 days from the date of delivery.

Segmentation and Targeting Strategy

Sell to Everyone

The first market segmentation strategy is the broadest: not defining a specific market. You attempt to sell to everyone. Although this sounds good and should result in the greatest sales, it is usually unrealistic. Because each group of consumers perceives their wants and needs differently, each one needs to be solicited with a specific message that will make this group remember and purchase your product. If a message is too general and vague, a broad range of consumers may see it, but no one group will remember and act on it.

Differentiated Marketing

The second approach to market segmentation is called *differentiated marketing*. It is the attempt to modify your product and marketing efforts in such a way that you solicit two or more segments simultaneously. The Microsoft Network—MSN—promotions are an excellent example. By using various ethnic groups, older and younger age groups, and women in its banner ads, commercials, magazines, and the like, Microsoft solicits several specific markets individually for its online service—often in the same advertisement.

Concentrated Marketing

The third and most limited segmentation strategy is called *concentrated marketing*. This is the selection of one or only a few closely related target segments. For example, BMW targets young, upwardly mobile professionals in its TV commercials, which stress appearance, performance and prestige.

■ Distribution Channels

The final step in preparing your marketing plan is to decide how you will sell your product or service, where you are going to locate your business and how you are going to get your product or service to the customer. The purpose of the distribution process is to deliver what the customer wants to a place he will buy it. Several of the more common distribution channels are described in this section.

Direct Sales

Direct sales are the most common form of distribution. Car dealerships are obvious examples. Other kinds of direct distribution companies range from the entrepreneurial Mary Kay to monolithic entertainment businesses such as Warner Bros. Each produces its own product line—cosmetics and feature films respectively—and bypasses the wholesaler, selling directly to consumers through its own retail outlets and franchises—entrepreneurial sales reps and theater chains respectively. The benefits of direct distribution are control over supply, control of distribution and quality, increased buying power, lower administrative costs and ability to capture profits that would have been earned by other companies at the various stages of distribution.

Indirect Sales

Indirect sales strategies related to brand image include extensive, selective and exclusive distribution. Indirect distribution is where a manufacturer sells to a wholesaler who sells to a retailer who ultimately sells to the customer. The majority of firms operates at one level and does not control the entire distribution chain because of a lack of expertise and capital.

Variations of indirect distribution channels include OEMs (Original Equipment Manufacturers), wholesale dealers (that specialize in, say, dry groceries and the like), and VARs (Value-Added Retailers). In the early stages of a new product, when cash is tight, OEMs can generate and build new sales, while in the growth stage, Dealers and VARs are needed.

Extensive

Often described as the "shotgun" approach, extensive distribution sells your product or service through as many retailers as possible without regard to image or competition. This type of channel works best for convenience goods such as soap, pencils, film, and other household goods. The idea is to sell through all responsible outlets where the customer would expect to find your product.

Selective

Selective distribution is the broad category between extensive and exclusive. You want to reach as many potential customers through as many responsible outlets as possible, but you want to maintain some type of image. This approach attempts to reach more than one customer profile or target market by selecting specific outlets with specific images and then matching product selection and promotion to that image. Good policy here includes avoiding outlets with bad credit, poor service, a bad customer image, and a poor location. Selective distribution differs from extensive in that it subscribes to the concept that 80% of a company's sales come from 20% of its customers. There is no need to sell your product through every retail outlet under this distribution strategy.

Exclusive

Exclusive distribution, often called "the rifle approach," is selling your product or service at a very limited number of retail outlets, either a single store or chain. An example of this approach would be Ralph Lauren apparel being originally sold in such department stores as Burdines and Lord & Taylors, not Sears or JCPenney—and before Ralph Lauren opened its successful chain or retail outlets and online store. The objective of exclusive distribution is to reach a single target market. It usually requires strong dealer loyalty and active sales support from the dealer. Exclusive distribution is "brand and image" conscious and is usually used in conjunction with a concentrated marketing strategy. In choosing this distribution strategy, it is important to avoid distributing to competing channels.

This strategy, of course, does not exclude spin-offs from the core product. Eyeware, for example, that have the brand name and cachet of Ralph Lauren, can be purchased in LensCrafters—but Polo clothes cannot.

OEM

The OEM sale has the lowest marketing cost and the highest real margin. Wide market exposure and a solid market penetration are possible. An OEM will often "bundle" or promote its product (e.g., software) or service (e.g., pet grooming plus vet care) with yours or pay a royalty on each product sold.

Dealers

Dealers add value to the product by providing floor space and end-user sales. Successful dealers prefer to buy from a distributor to minimize their vendor list. They want consolidated billing and dependable deliveries. Advertising and promoting your product will ensure dealer interest.

VARs

A VAR (Value-Added Reseller) develops customer loyalty by "added value" to your product. A consultant is a good example of a VAR. A VAR does not make a product, but rather provides a service in addition to your product that is considered an extra value to the customer. A close and personal relationship along with training, referrals and regular communication help make VARs a good choice for channel distribution.

Internet

Many kinds of businesses—from large catalog companies such as L.L. Bean to sole proprietor "eBay stores"—use a website to attract, inform, and sell to customers. During the Holiday season of 2005, records were made for online shopping. Customers have clearly become comfortable and more confident in making secure online transactions.

Controversy, however, still surrounds unsolicited email advertising to millions of people, a.k.a. "spamming." While this may appear to be a great way to reach millions, if the questionable ethics and cat-and-mouse games with filter technology are not an inhibition, the multimillion dollar judgments that Microsoft and other Internet service providers are winning should be. Expect to pay your own way in this kind of business because most lenders will not want their "good name" associated with built-in bad reputation.

Other Kinds of Distribution Channels

Home shopping on cable television is still an excellent way to market and sell small products such as jewelry, convenience tools (such as those Popeil kitchen aids), and the like.

Small product businesses such as crafts have many options, including consignment sales, holiday fairs, art fairs, flea markets, craft brokers, mail order, trade shows, and craft malls. The BizPlanBuilder Handbook covers this kind of business and its distribution strategies in detail.

■ **Advertising and Promotion**

Doing business without advertising is like winking at a girl in the dark.
You know what you are doing, but nobody else does.
— *Steuart H. Britt*

Promotion

The goals of promotion are simple: to inform, to persuade and to remind.

Promotion includes advertising, publicity or public relations, personal selling, and sales promotions. The promotional strategy you choose will be determined by marketing decisions you have already made. The purpose of a promotion is to tell potential customers that you have a product or service that can satisfy their demands, to convince those potential customers to buy from you and to successfully compete with other, similar businesses. Your message will depend on the target market you identify and how that market will perceive your message.

Advertising

Advertising is sending impersonal messages to selected large audiences for the purpose of soliciting or informing consumers. This includes such forms as the Internet, television, radio, print, direct mail, email, outdoor billboards, signs on mass transit vehicles, point-of-purchase displays in stores and ads in the "yellow pages." Which medium you choose is based on the target market and cost per person receiving the advertisement. In advertising, no individual representing your business is communicating directly with your potential customer. As a consequence, advertising messages are limited to one-way communications. Advertising works well when your target market strategy is to solicit business from a broad market. However, it can become quite specific when you choose local media such as newspapers and radio and television airtime.

Sales Promotion

A sales promotion is marketing stimuli (messages) used to generate demand for your product or service. The purpose of a sales promotion is to convince those potential customers to buy from you immediately.

Examples of sales promotions targeted at consumers include special aisle displays, samples, coupons, contests, banners, and free gifts. Promotions are also aimed at wholesalers and internal salespeople and can include contests, sales aids, meetings, catalogs, price promotions, and trade shows.

Personal Selling

Personal selling is defined as a "person-to-person sales" presentation. The advantage of this approach is that it allows for two-way communication between your representative and your potential customer. Although personal selling generally results in more sales directly related to the promotional efforts, it is a very expensive form of promotion. Another disadvantage is that it can limit the size of your potential target market segment.

Some types of direct selling include the "canned" presentation, where a sales representative recites a memorized sales pitch to the customer. Although this allows you more control over what message the customer receives, it does not allow for an open channel of communication such as the "feature versus benefit" approach, and often discourages potential customers. In feature versus benefit selling, your representative spends time asking the customer what his specific wants and needs are. He or she then attempts to show the customer how your business can satisfy those wants and needs better than other competitors. This type of sales approach usually leaves the customer feeling satisfied with his decision. If there are any misunderstandings or reservations, your salesperson can handle them before closing the sale. Feature versus benefit direct selling is also an excellent opportunity for you to gain valuable insight into the wants and needs of your target market, to track changes in customer demand, and to collect good feedback on performance.

Deciding which type of sales approach to choose determines what type of sales force you must hire. These decisions very closely follow your decision about distribution. You have the choice of hiring a captive direct sales force or using independent sales representatives who represent your company as well as other companies. If you choose independent representatives, your expenses will be lower, but you have less control over the representation of your company and products. If he or she is unprofessional or chooses to emphasize another product that will earn him a higher income, the sales and reputation of your business could suffer. With a captive direct sales force, you have increased expenses for employee salaries and benefits, such as Social Security, pensions, and medical insurance. Your choice of compensation includes salary, commission, or some combination of both.

Personal selling is targeted directly at the final consumer, whereas advertising, publicity and public relations are aimed at a mass or large target audience.

Advertising Budget

Your plan needs to include your advertising and promotional budget. Your investor wants to know how much it costs to launch or maintain sales, if those costs are reasonable in comparison to the projected gains, what your competition is spending, and how this budget compares to your other budget factors. Details of your promotional budget are internal documents meant to guide your day-to-day operations. Here, you simply summarize the data. Attach any details you feel would boost your investor's confidence in the Supporting Documents section.

There are four common methods for calculating an advertising and promotions budget. They are discussed in the following subsections.

Marginal

The first method is the marginal approach and can be difficult to implement. The marginal approach is spending to the point where the last expenditure on advertising equals the net profit on sales generated by that advertisement (usually, large corporations use this approach).

Available Funds

A second method for determining how much to spend on advertising is the available funds approach, which is spending whatever you can afford. Although probably the most commonly used method, available funds are also the most conservative. The more you spend on effective advertising, the more sales you will generate. In other words, if you make the investment in quality advertising, you will generate the sales to pay for the advertising.

Budgetary

The next method to determine the amount to be spent on advertising is the budgetary approach—that is, spending a percentage of projected sales on advertising. If you want sales to reach a certain level next year, you need to spend a certain percentage on advertising during the year.

"Match dollar for dollar"

The final approach is to match "dollar for dollar" what your competition is spending. This method is based on the assumption that equal spending will at least keep you and the competition equal in terms of sales levels and market shares.

Measuring Your Success

Plan to measure the success of your advertising budget. Simple metrics can be used such as the number of responses you get or the increase in sales due correlated to responses. You can measure events by the attendance and by inquiries made afterward that result in sales. BizPlanBuilder, for example, uses a "Priority Code" or "Discount Code"—supplied in its advertisements—to track how effective these ads are through its online checkout system.

■ Public Relations

Publicity is often referred to as *public relations*. Publicity is information about your product or company that is not a direct message from you to the potential customer. It is usually reported by an independent party. You do not directly pay for publicity, but its value to you in terms of sales can be dramatic. An example of publicity is the weekly food column in the newspaper. If you own a restaurant, you do not pay for a restaurant review, but information about your business, food and service is reported to the public. Publicity can be either good or bad, and you have little control over what is reported. The review that raves about the quality service at your restaurant can double sales overnight.

The importance of publicity is underscored in the BizPlanBuilder program. It includes template documents in the Supporting Documents and Managing Your Business masters for getting free publicity and creating a press release. You can also click the **More Tools** button on the BizPlanBuilder toolbar to access additional JIAN products designed specifically for public relations planning.

Major Sales Announcements

Major agreements should be written up and released to selected media as soon as possible after they are signed. Ideally, these would be joint announcements. At the same time, a shortened version of the release should be mailed to all internal and external sales organizations.

Press Releases

Prepare press releases on the entire product line/service area for each new product introduction, technical development, participation in a major event, awards/recognition for product/personnel excellence/performance, and the like. Include an 8 × 10 black-and-white glossy photo of your product or an interesting demo of your service that editors will probably pick up at trade shows, "homeramas," and similar venues.

Use trade shows as another method for maintaining a high profile with the editors of key target media. If a major product announcement is feasible at a show, plan the announcement well in advance. However, because the major publications send their editors to the major shows, an opportunity exists to schedule short interviews between key personnel and selected reporters and editors. These mini-interviews can be used in lieu of the editorial visit (described below), or as opportunities to give editors a company or product update from a chief executive's point of view.

Editorial Visits

Inviting the most influential reporters and editors from targeted publications for a visit is important in maintaining high visibility in the marketplace. During the visit, each editor should receive a complete facility tour, product briefing and an opportunity to interview the chairperson, president, product designer and marketing manager. If logistics or timing is a problem with the interviews, then these could possibly be arranged at the major trade shows.

Trade Shows

Trade shows are also a valuable way to evaluate the competition and to expand your knowledge of other products in your industry. The following factors should be taken into consideration when selecting which trade shows to attend:

- Target audience of the show; will this get the message to our target market?

- Geographic location; a good mix of shows around the country

- Time frame; preferably no more than one show each month

- Past experience, if any, with the show

- Participation in someone else's booth

A typical face-to-face sales call costs over $200 these days. At a trade show you enjoy having your full demo set up, all your brochures ready to go, your salespeople and managers are all there . . . and the prospects come to you! The trick is choosing which show to attend and planning to maximize your investment. The tradeshow media kit should include all the appropriate demographic and psychographic information—just like a magazine—so you calculate approximately how many of the right people might come by your booth. What's the cost of the lead, the value of being able to give your full pitch right there, the value of your visibility at the show, and so on? Just make sure you have a plan to follow up on your prospects (don't laugh, a lot of companies lose it right here) or you're wasting your time and money right from the start.

List Management

List management is used to target your customers via a database containing names and addresses of your customer or potential customers. Customer lists can be purchased for target markets, but are more effective if developed in-house. Registration cards and periodic surveys will help you build your customer list and measure the success of your marketing activities by providing a historical profile of your customer.

Internal/External Newsletter

An internal or external newsletter serves as an informational piece for internal personnel, the sales force and key customers. It includes sections covering each major department or organization within the company, such as sales, marketing, manufacturing, and R&D, as well as a message from the executive staff. It also highlights milestones such as key sales stories, successful customer applications, significant marketing events and product development news.

■ Marketing Plan Checklist

√ How are you positioning your product and/or company?

√ How are you determining the price for your product?

√ Who are you planning to sell your product to?

√ What type of distribution channel(s) do you plan to use?

√ What type of advertising and promotion are you planning to use?

√ How much money do you plan to spend on advertising and promotions?

√ How can public relations be used in selling your product and/or company?

■ BizPlanBuildercise 3.6: Review the Marketing Strategy Template

Open and review the Marketing Strategy/Plan template of your business plan.

1. Launch BizPlanBuilder if necessary.

2. Choose to work on the LogaTorial example or your own business plan.

3. Double-click Marketing Strategy in the current plan area of the Item list. (Click **OK** to close the warning window if necessary.)

4. Maximize the Document pane as desired.

5. Review the component thoroughly by scrolling through the template document and reading its content, placeholders, and Expert Comments.

6. Notice the length of your template and how it is subdivided. For example, Internet marketing, so important to the success of event he smallest venture now, can have a special emphasis and cover topics such as search engine keywords, email marketing, and so on. (See illustration below.) A template can run from two pages, as in the case of the Service/Bank Loan plan, to over 10 pages for the more detailed Retail, Internet , and Angel/VC plans, which have most of the features discussed in this section.

Keyword Search section in the Internet Plan's Market Strategy template.

Key-Word Search

Whenever anyone uses a popular search engine to search for '[key words relative to your product or service]' in Google, Overture, Yahoo!, Lycos, Excite, AltaVista, an advertisement / link to LogaTorial Prepress Service's website should appear.

❖ Try this software: http://www.goodkeywords.com, you can download a free software product that enables you to enter your keywords so you can see how many times they have been searched in the past month(s). This may be the most credible and timely market research available today.

According to recent search engine statistics (using the Overture keyword analysis tools), these keywords produce the following number of inquiries over the past [xx] months:

- Employee   25,091
- Employee background check   4,441
- Restaurant business plan   3,309
- Xxx0,000
- Xxx0,000
- Xxx0,000

❖ You can also use this method to determine better words to use in your advertising copy. For example, 'business consultant' is requested 17,772 times while 'business expert' is requested 77 times. Which word would you use if you were writing an ad or direct mail piece to reach business consultants?

7. If desired, close BizPlanBuilder when you are done.

Optional Exercise. Many of the templates in your BizPlanBuilder business plan have marketing-oriented features. Three of the masters, for example, contain a separate Internet Strategy template. The Market Opportunity template can be appended to the Market Analysis to give your narrative a quick snapshot of your access to potential customers.

■ Review Questions 3.6

1. Why is price one of the most effective marketing tools? What should price be based on?

_____

_____

_____

_____

2. What are the pros and cons of using email for an advertising campaign? Even if you are against "spam" and "spammers" in principle, if it could sell more product or services, would you use email to reach customers?

_____

_____

_____

_____

_____

3. Your firm is makes gourmet chipotle dog "yummies." What do you recommend for the distribution strategy: direct or indirect? Extensive or exclusive?

_____

_____

_____

_____

_____

4. Nell Cohen is considering *Cigar Aficionado* as a possible advertising medium for her home wine cellar service. She calls the magazine to request its media kit. What information should she expect to receive?

_____

_____

_____

_____

_____

5. How are public relations and publicity different from advertising? In what situations are public relations most beneficial?

_____

_____

_____

_____

6. Why do companies spend time and money attending trade shows as exhibitors of products or services?

_____

_____

_____

_____

■ Activities 3.6

1. Using the Marketing Strategy component of a BizPlanBuilder template reviewed in BizPlanBuildercise 3.6, describe the basic marketing plan, sales strategy, and positioning strategy for your proposed venture. (As an alternate activity, perform this activity with the Internet [Marketing] Strategy component if your plan has one.)

2. Assume your company is making a phenomenal new aftermarket wiper blade for cars and trucks. The wiper material works better and lasts longer than anything on the market, but the car manufacturers are not interested in your product. Using the Distribution Channels section of the Marketing Strategy component, describe how you would distribute this product. Complete this section through the Returns and Adjustments Policy section.

3. Using the Advertising and Promotion section, describe the promotion strategy for your proposed product or service. (Stop at the Preliminary Media Schedule section.)

4. Contact a radio or TV station, a magazine, or a newspaper, and ask for a media kit including the Standard Rate and Data Sheet. How much might your proposed firm spend with this one media outlet in a one-year period? (As a variation on this activity, obtain a media kit for Web advertising using popup, banner ads, and nonspam, legitimate email messages.)

In the end, all business operations can be reduced to three words: people, product, and profits.
—*Lee Iacocca*

Operations

How you describe the facilities, staffing, product and service fulfillment, and the technology that your venture requires for success is now a focal point even in the most basic business plan. The readers of its narrative components will be looking for how you intend to operate and *manage* operations before they write any checks or make any investment that turns your plan into a real business. You cannot afford to be vague—just as you cannot fudge on the financials, which will be discussed in the next part of this book.

The following sections will provide you with the basic guidelines for preparing BizPlanBuilder's Operations templates. These include facilities, staff, product and service fulfillment, and technology (with an emphasis on IT). Also covered are such issues as packaging, transportation, returns and adjustments policy, and so on.

■ Facilities

Your facility—or facilities—can be anything from a head office to a factory to a warehouse to retail locations. In the case of dry cleaning firm, they can include the plant or plants if you intend to have separate facilities for clothes, drapes, carpets, and son on. Likewise, you may want separate drop-off and delivery locations in your *area of operations*. If you are setting up a pizza chain, you may have one set of facilities to manufacture your sauce, dough, and salads, and another set to serve and sell the product, namely, a chain of restaurants.

The size, number, and scope of facilities is as large or small as you want to be. If you are Molly LeDier of LogaTorial, your facilities may be a small office in a room across the hall from the bedroom. (What a tough commute she has!). But even for the small service or crafts business, some variation on the following variables has to be considered:

- Room and cost for expansion

- Land (even space in your home) and construction costs

- Location-location-location—which means where are you going to put up your stores and services centers, even where you are going to locate your home office

- Transportation cost and route access for common carrier

- Risks and insurance

- Packaging and material costs and availability

- Labor pool availability, skills, costs

- Local ordinances, licensing and permit requirements

- Government assistance (roads, training, exemptions, etc.)

- Government restrictions and requirements (OSHA, NLRB, etc.)

- Community attitudes toward business and manufacturing

- Continued operating costs (utilities, communications, etc.)

- Management—who manages operations and what—meaning IT software

■ Staffing

People are one of the most significant resources for your business. Assessing the required number of people and their skills, how and when they will be trained, and who will hire and manage them is important to your product/service—and operations—strategy.

Another important consideration is training and learning curves for your staff. Operations management (OM) is another.

You will also need to describe management in your plan narrative—the kinds of expertise you will need and its cost. Your business plan must state how you intend to manage your venture's operations. This is true even if you are a freelancer or an entrepreneur with more than just sales managers. In addition to the Management template, which describes the members of your management team and how the contribute to the profitability. In the Staffing section of the Operations template, you can integrate how your managers will interact and oversee your staffing needs, training, and other human resource issues.

■ Technology

The BizPlanBuilder comments in its Operations templates discuss an important consideration for your venture: your company's "technology stack." This IT jargon and you can expect an investor who is looking over your business plan to ask, "So, what is your technology stack?"—or something like that, such as "IT infrastructure." As impressive as they may be trying to sound, you still need to impress them with an authentic understanding of how you intend to operate in this important dimension of any modern business.

A "technology stack" is the hard- and software that runs your business operations and backs up and restores your data. It ranges from storage devices to the databases and front and back office databases and enterprise solution software (think Oracle, Informix, Sybase, Microsoft, SAP) to application servers (like the Windows application server and systems for ERP, e-commerce, e-mail, and back-office services). In addition, you may want to seek consultants—as important as your legal and financial advisors—in preparing the IT component of your business plan narrative.

This section of the business plan also means traditional technology, from postal meters to conveyor belts to the kind of delivery vans you intend to use. That is, whatever technology is applicable to make your operations work and what these technologies will cost vis-à-vis the profits that your business plan projects.

■ Fulfillment

Product and service fulfillment is an important part of customer satisfaction—and you conceptualize and explain it in your business plan will, of course, *satisfy* the questions that your readers will have about this feature of your business. Providing a channel to monitor and manage the delivery. For example, if your business depends on shipping catalogue orders or selling a service and getting it to where the client is—which can be anywhere now, from the home to the computer desktop to a parking space in the airport if your business is a mobile carwash.

The readers—the evaluators—of your business plan will want to know things about billing, warranty, and repair of your products or restitution if your service is dissatisfactory. That is, how will you ensure customer satisfaction and repeat business?

Many businesses rely on outside providers of marketing and sales, shipping, IT service providers, and the like. If you intend to solve some of your operations problems with outside fulfillment vendors, you will need to detail that as well as its costs and benefits in your business plan. This means getting a menu of services and their costs, which can be incorporated into the Operations section of your plan or as a support document.

■ Other Considerations

Customer service and support are also part of operations. The Operations part of the business plan narrative should cover how you intend to server your clients (e.g., how you intend to pick up and deliver to them, how you intend to handle warranties and refunds, and so on).

How your business interacts with the environment is also an operations consideration. Some BizPlanBuilder masters have a special *Environment* template to describe this facet. If you intend to buy property, expect to have it evaluated for any violations by the previous owner regarding chemical spills and illegal disposal. Your new venture does not need to be hamstrung by inheriting someone else's problem. A *Risk* template is also provided for describing how your venture interacts with the legal environment. Both of these templates expand on what Operations covers.

If you intend to make or market a product—and using, for example, the Angel/VC plan—a *Manufacturing* section in your Operations narrative is probably necessary. This is where you would justify why you want to manufacture domestically or outsource. Why you need your own facilities or why you would need to contract others to make what you want to sell.

■ Operations Checklist

√ What will your present and future space requirements be?

√ Do you need to purchase real estate?

√ Do you need to build, convert, or rent facilities?

√ What kinds of staffing will you need? What training will they need and what will be its costs and learning curve?

√ Management? What kind of background and expertise do you need?

√ What kind of "technology stack" do you need?

√ Do you need to purchase IT equipment and services, including IT consultants?

√ Where will your stores and service centers be located?

√ Will warehouses be used? If so, where and what size? What inventory levels will be carried?

√ Do you need to describe any kind of manufacturing or service process?

√ Are their any environmental impacts that effect operations?

√ Where will distribution centers be located?

√ What packaging and handling equipment will be used and who will supply it?

√ What special equipment, if any, will be needed such as trucks, tractors, etc.?

√ How will you fulfill orders for products or services?

√ Will you contract for outside fulfillment vendors?

■ BizPlanBuildercise 3.7: Review the Operations Template

Open and review the Operations template of your business plan.

1. Launch BizPlanBuilder if necessary.

2. Choose to work on the LogaTorial example or your own business plan.

3. Double-click ⬡ Operations in the current plan area of the Item list. (Click **OK** to close the warning window if necessary.)

4. Maximize the Document pane as desired.

5. Review the component thoroughly by scrolling through the template document and reading its content, placeholders, and Expert Comments. (See illustration on next page.)

6. If desired, close BizPlanBuilder.

Optional Exercise. Open and review an Environment template in one of the template masters. This is an optional part of the business plan narrative that you may want to include with your business plan after the Operations part or as a supplement. Many investors, lenders—and grant resources if you are seeking certain kinds of private or government funds—like to participate in financing businesses that take an active part in environmental sustainability. Even a small business can utilize this component. Molly LeDier's prepress business uses a lot of copy paper and her plan to recycle 100% of her waste is going to be stated in her business plan supplement. She is also going to use environmentally friendly facilities, lighting, transportation, and the like in her day-to-day operations.

> **The Manufacturing section of the Angel/VC plan's Operations template. Here and in some of the other templates, you may need to deal with controversial issues that affect your business plan and how it is received.**

Manufacturing

❖ As much as I want to promote and support America, I must advise you that most investors and lenders expect you to be outsourcing your manufacturing to China. (...hate to say this, but we must do what we can to assure our success and return to our investors.) It's just cheaper and getting cheaper every day. There will be more for Americans to do—we just need to rethink, rekindle and reconnect...

❖ American jobs are created everyday as a result of doing business with China. More and more entrepreneurs are able to set up their own businesses because of the great pricing overseas. We have just made an evolution from the factories to the office.

The Company has numerous sources for product manufacturing—Including both domestic as well as offshore sources in China. (We [must/are] set up this way to both minimize our costs and allow for the flexibility of rapid production without the long shipping lead time from overseas if/when needed...

The factory monthly production capacity is [xxx] units per day, [xxx] units per month. Production can be ramped up within 6 months to [xxx] units per month if needed.

We have audited our production lines in China and have verified that they are capable of manufacturing the product to our standard, and we are only using ISO 9002 approved factories to assure consistency. The factory we which we have our alliance has all of the necessary approvals for our products: UL, FDA, CE, ISO, Child Labor Compliant, etc. They are located near the Shanghai/Ningbo/Hong Kong port for convenient exportation.

■ Review Questions 3.7

1. List five variables that affect facilities.

_____

_____

_____

_____

2. Why is staff training part of operations? Why would it make sense to include it in a business plan?

_____

_____

_____

_____

3. What kind of "technology stack" would a small, home-office business require?

_____

_____

_____

_____

4. What kind of information from an outside fulfillment provider would you need for your supporting documentation?

_____

_____

_____

_____

■ Activities 3.7

1. Meeting the needs of your customers determines how and where you locate your business and its satellites. After you have reviewed the Operations template in BizPlanBuildercise 3.7, draft in notes or directly in the template, how you would locate your business. Whether you have several locations or one—even if you are home "officed"—how would technology increase the operational scope of your location?

2. The Operations part of the business plan narrative requires an explanation of how you intend to use personal computers, servers, websites, and the like to operate your business from the inside and how it interacts with your clients and other businesses (either as suppliers or clients). Search the Internet for articles and diagrams that show this complex process (Keywords: **internet + technology + solution**, and so on).

3. Facilities and staffing are separate sections in the Operations template. How would you break these down into needs for a brew pub-type business? What kind of facilities would you need (kitchen, brewery, etc.)? What kind of staffing would you need (a manager, a brewmaster, cooks, servers, et al.)? In the imaginary role of a consultant, how would you help an entrepreneur fill out this part of his or her business plan narrative? You can do this activity with a list of solutions or a list of problems and questions. Even if this is not the business you intend to run, the process of finding the information is the real lesson of this activity.

4. If you are starting a service business, would you delete the Returns & Adjustments Policy section of Operations template—or would you revise it to explain how you would fulfill the guaranteed quality of your service?

This was the Promised Land, and still it is.

—*Hart Crane*

Part 4: Completing the Financial Plan

BizPlanBuilder helps you to both understand—and build—that part of you business plan simply called the "financials." The financial plan is a summary of your business's financial history—past and present if they exist—and the financial projections about the future and the assumptions upon which they are based. This tells your investors, the bankers, angels, and other stakeholders (1) how much funding you need, (2) what you need it for, and (3) how and when you intend to pay it back.

For a startup company, the financial plan becomes a living tool. Its projections can be compared with real-world results so that you can adjust your business's course before serious financial problems result.

While the financial plan is primarily a narrative piece in your plan, it is customary to include spreadsheets and other supporting documents. This way, reviewers can see your data and hand it over to their number crunchers—if necessary—to see if your conclusions are sound. You can provide spreadsheets for the basic startup costs and projected profit (and loss) of your venture for its first year of operation. If you require large sums and your business is big enough, exhaustive detail is needed. Standard accounting spreadsheets are usually required for any loan applications. These can include anticipated Return on Investment (ROI) over three years, a capital equipment and supply list, balance sheet, break-even analysis, pro forma income projections—given as a profit and loss statement—and pro forma cash flow. The income statement and cash flow projections can a multiyear summary, detailed by month for the first year and detailed by quarter for subsequent years. And much of this information goes into what you write in the Financial Plan, which can be both narratives and illustrative charts and tables.

These financials come predesigned in BizPlanBuilder's templates. The Comprehensive Model features workbooks that drive a company's numbers based upon percentages of revenue. Spending can be adjusted depending upon revenue. You can even use these models as part of the process of writing your narrative by generating projected financial statements. These *numbers* reflect the goals and information that will guide how you "talk up" the venture in the narrative and how you enter the real projections into your spreadsheets.

No matter what kind of business you are planning to start, BizPlanBuilder has a set of Microsoft Excel worksheets as well as Word document templates that introduce the financials with a narrative outline. Angel/VC, Retail, and Internet plans use Financial Plan *and* Capital Requirements templates. The Service/Bank Loan features a Financial Plan template. These provide you with a narrative form that can include summaries of your business's financial history (if applicable), your financial projections, and the assumptions you based them on, your projected capital requirements and how the capital will be used, and your plan to repay your lenders and investors. The Exit Strategy template logically follows the financials—it is where you project how you are paid back when your venture can be converted into an IPO. The financials can be further augmented with a Personal Financial Statement from the library of Supporting Documents templates in BizPlanBuilder—this is necessary when you put up your own money as well.

This part of *BizPlanBuilder Express* covers:

Purpose of a Financial Plan

Financial Statement Overviews

Projecting Financial Statements

Using the Financial Plan Spreadsheets

Printing the Financial Statements

Customizing the Financial Statements

Financial Plan Narrative Text

Using BizPlanBuilder's Financial Plan Masters

▶ **Learning Objectives**

After Completing Part 4, you should be able to:

1. Understand the purpose of your financial plan
2. Learn the common components of a financial statement
3. Project financial statements for your business venture
4. Understand the capital requirements for your startup, firm expansion, or reorganization
5. Understand the purpose of the financial plan narrative
6. Locate and open applicable financial plan templates in BizPlanBuilder

> **You should prepare your BizPlanBuilder worksheets in cooperation and with the advice of your accountant or financial adviser.**
>
> **It is beyond the scope of this course to actually enter data in the Excel worksheets used in the BizPlanBuilder financials. The following discussion is limited to a general survey of the financial plan and the versatility of BizPlanBuilder's powerful Microsoft Excel workbooks.**

■ The Purpose of a Financial Plan

It is recommended that you start writing your narrative first. There is, for lack of a better description, a creative freedom to think and express your business ideas without the purse strings attached. Nevertheless, the narrative and the financials of a business plan are synergistic—they inform the preparation of each other. There is also a legal dimension. Bear in mind that everything you write will need to be funded and in the post-Enron and WorldCom world, the world of Sarbanes-Oxley and stringent accounting laws and guidelines, you must prepare a sound financial plan.

Projected financial statements are the tools used to determine if a business is viable and what capital will be required for startup. The financial statements model the financial operation of a business in the same way that you might model a production process or inventory flow. When used to forecast your business's capital requirements, these statements are often referred to as financial projections or pro forma statements. When completed, these projected financial statements should be included in the Financial Models or Supporting Documents component of your business plan—along with your historical financial statements if applicable. In BizPlanBuilder, these are Microsoft Excel worksheets—which provide you with a user-friendly way of working with simple and complex financial spreadsheets. (These can even be linked or special pasted as tables in your Microsoft Word document narrative that always reflect the current numbers in the worksheets.)[*]

Although you are probably not an accountant, it is important that you understand some basic goals and principles of accounting and some of the methods and statements accountants use for recording financial information. The more you understand about financial statements, how to project them, and how to analyze them, the more reasonable and valuable your projected statements will be. As a result, the financial plan portion of your business plan will be more thorough, which may assist you in obtaining financing.

The following section assumes you understand some basic accounting principles, the most common financial statements and several financial analysis methods. You may need to review a basic introductory accounting textbook. If you have additional or specific accounting questions, we suggest you consult your accountant or financial advisor.

■ Financial Statements Overviews

This section discusses the function of each of the most common financial statements and their key components.

What Are Financial Statements?

Basically, financial statements are standardized forms developed by accountants and financial managers to record business transactions. Financial statements are designed to reflect standard accounting practices and follow a fundamental principle of accounting: matching costs and expenses with the revenues they created. In order for costs and expenses to be matched with revenues, accountants devised what is known as the double entry system of accounting.

What Are the Financial Statements Templates?

BizPlanBuilder includes a set of financial spreadsheet Masters to help you produce financial statements in support of your business plan. Using the Excel spreadsheet processor, you edit the templates with your own financial data.

In BizPlanBuilder, you can use the individual Basic Financial Statements spreadsheets. If your business venture requires a more detailed set of spreadsheets, you can use either Intermediate or Comprehensive financial models. These highly automated Excel workbooks are integrated financials in which the

---

[*] It is assumed that you can operate the basic features of the Microsoft Excel versions supported by BizPlanBuilder. If you need assistance, see your instructor, accountant, or another practitioner who is experienced with spreadsheet applications. Also, consult Appendix D, Using Microsoft Word and Excel.

Excel spreadsheets are linked together. If you change one number, any corresponding cell will be updated. Other features are discussed later.

A wide selection of financial statements is provided in BizPlanBuilder. You may not need or want to include all of them in your business plan. Only prepare and include the financial statements that are appropriate for your needs.

In the Item List (see below), scroll down to locate the three levels of financial templates that come with BizPlanBuilder.

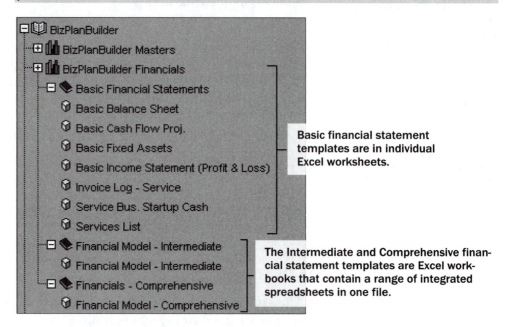

Basic financial statement templates are in individual Excel worksheets.

The Intermediate and Comprehensive financial statement templates are Excel workbooks that contain a range of integrated spreadsheets in one file.

An assumption is any condition that you believe to be true based on research and analysis that determines how much money you need to generate profit for a new business or additional profit for an existing business venture. There are other kinds of business assumptions (legal, marketing, management, etc.). The assumptions expressed in your financials are how much things will cost to make a profit. This can be people and space, human resources, capital to buy equipment, marketing, R&D, enterprise software, and so on. BizPlanBuilder's Comprehensive financial model contains worksheets to develop these assumptions, which are then turned into the words that form the narrative of your plan. The spreadsheets will back you up when you face challenges from investors, bankers, and others—what numbers go in at the beginning and how did you arrive at them among other questions.

The Basic Assumptions worksheet in BizPlanBuilder workbooks does not express the same thing—only a small part. This worksheet is where you enter basic data for identifying your company, stock issuance, products and services and what they cost to generate profit ("profit centers"). The exact content can vary. See the *BizPlanBuilder Handbook* for more information.

Gross Profit Analysis Statement

The Gross Profit Analysis statement presents a breakdown of the month-by-month sales, cost of goods sold, and gross profit for each product or product line. It calculates the monthly gross profit for each sales item—which can also be a service—by subtracting the monthly costs for Material, Labor, and Fixed Cost of Goods & Services for each item from the monthly sales for each item. The Gross Profit Analysis can assist you in determining the profitability of individual products—or service packages—and how they contribute to your total gross profit.

In the Financial Plan narrative document of the Angel/VC master, for example, information generated by Gross Profit Analysis statement is entered into a simplified table—while a more detailed spreadsheet can be placed in either the Intermediate or Comprehensive Financial Model. For smaller business ventures using the Basic Income Statement, the gross revenue numbers are entered here—and then drawn from to supply information for the cash reserves section of the narrative's Financial Plan document.

Budget Statements

Budget Statements presents a month-by-month projection of revenues and expenses over a one-year period. Your budget is the foundation for projecting your other financial statements. It presents a more detailed accounting of your expenses than on an Income Statement (discussed next). On a budget, expense details are usually grouped by department or functional area, such as Sales and Marketing and cost of goods sold.

Obviously, a budget statement is for complex business ventures and is a prominent feature of the Comprehensive Model workbook. For example, the Financial Plan of the Angel/VC master includes a subsection for the Budget in its narrative, underneath the heading Gross Profit Analysis. BizPlanBuilder advises that the budget statement is for internal purposes and is not normally required for most business plans. The same information can be found—or be informed by detailed budget statements—in the Income Statement or Cash Flow Projection, which is usually sufficient and is expressed in both narrative and spreadsheet form in BizPlanBuilder. Nevertheless, the budget statement should be on hand during any exhaustive presentation of the plan.

Income Statement

The Income Statement (also known as a statement of operations, or a profit & loss or P&L statement) summarizes the revenue and expense projections on a monthly basis for one year or an annual basis for several years. Like the budget, it presents sales, cost of goods sold (COGS), gross profit, operating expenses by category totals only, such as Sales and Marketing, General and Administrative, and Research and Development (R&D), income from operations, other income and expenses, income taxes, and net income. You should calculate year one income statement for each month, and then calculate three to five years of annual statements.

The Income Statement is normally used in place of budget statements within a business plan and whenever financial statements are issued to potential lenders and investors. When you review issues such as operating expenses with people outside your company, the income statement format helps focus the discussion on the reasonableness of category expenses in total (such as General and Administrative), instead of individual expenses (such as Postage or Telephone).

The Service/Bank Loan master includes an Income Statement section in the Financial Plan document. The Basic Income Statement (Profit & Loss) workbook provides enough detail for small and medium product or service business ventures.

> The Basic Income Statement shown below comes with two sheets. One is designed for service companies. The other is designed for product companies. Retail entrepreneurs can choose which one best suits their needs.

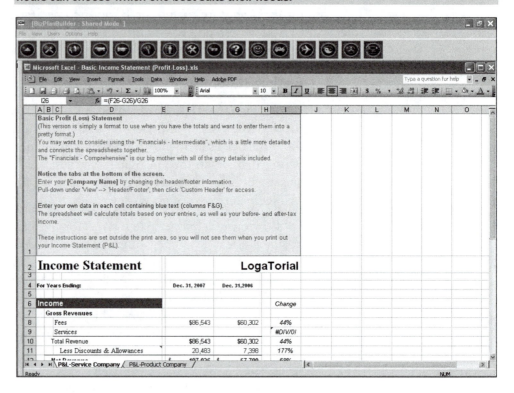

Break-Even Analysis Statement

The Break-Even Analysis Statement can assist you in predicting the effect of changes in costs and sales levels on the profitability of your business. This statement is used as an internal tool to test the sensitivity of your sales projections and the effects of management decisions regarding expenditures. The format of a break-even analysis statement can vary. One common monthly format uses the budget as its foundation, but separates all expenses into fixed or variable categories. Then it calculates the Contribution Margin, Break-Even Sales Volume and Sales Volume Above Break-Even for each month of your budget year.

> Costs or expenses are considered variable in nature if they vary directly with changes in sales volume, such as material and labor costs. Costs or expenses are considered fixed if they stay about the same as sales volume changes, such as rent or vice president salaries.

Cash Flow Statement

The Cash Flow Statement, also known as a Statement of Changes in Financial Position, summarizes your cash-related activities on a monthly basis for one year, or an annual basis for several years. Basically, cash flows statements show where your cash came from and where it went. The format of a cash flows statement can vary, but it often begins with the net income from your budget or income statement, then shows adjustments for items that do not involve cash (such as payables and depreciation); other nonoperational sources and applications of cash are listed next (such as fixed asset purchases and financing proceeds and payments), then the net cash balance is calculated.

The Cash Flow Statement is a feature of the Financial Plan narrative and its spreadsheet is included with the other summary financials in the Financial Models. The more detailed cash flow projection worksheets are provided in the Intermediate and Comprehensive workbooks. The cash flow worksheets in the Comprehensive financial statements template can cover up to five years.

Smaller business startups will typically not require this kind of information. However, in the Service/Bank Loan master, a Cash Reserves section exists in the narrative to identify the source of cash flow and project the cash reserves on hand after operating expenses. A Basic Cash Flow Projection worksheet (designed for either portrait or landscape printout) is provided in BizPlanBuilder's master templates, and it shows these projections on a monthly basis for one year.

Balance Sheet

The Balance Sheet, also known as a Statement of Financial Position, shows the financial position of your business at the end of a period, such as the end of a month or the end of a year—or a period of years. The income statement shows your sales revenue and related expenses for a time period resulting in your net income (or loss) for the period, which then becomes the increase (or decrease) in equity in your balance sheet. The balance sheet represents a "snapshot" of your company's resulting financial position, encompassing everything your company owns (Assets), owes (Liabilities) and the equity of the owner(s). The balances are a snapshot because they reflect your position on a specific day, not what has occurred over a period of time.

The balance sheet is divided into two parts which must always equal each other:

$$\text{Assets} = \text{Liabilities} + \text{Equity}$$

BizPlanBuilder's three financial plan models provide several levels of detail for this component. The Basic Balance Sheet has worksheets designed for a sole-proprietor business, a corporation, and a partnership. The automated Balance Sheets in the Intermediate and Comprehensive financial models are filled out by information that is entered into other worksheets in their respective Excel workbooks. These workbooks feed the assumptions you make and in your Financial Plan, you use them to support a commentary on any large or unusual items, such as other current assets, other assets, other accounts payable, or accrued liabilities.

Assets

Assets are those items your company owns. On a balance sheet, assets are commonly grouped into Current Assets, Fixed Assets and Other Assets categories.

The Basic Financial Statements includes a Fixed Assets Schedule (below) designed for typical small or home office businesses.

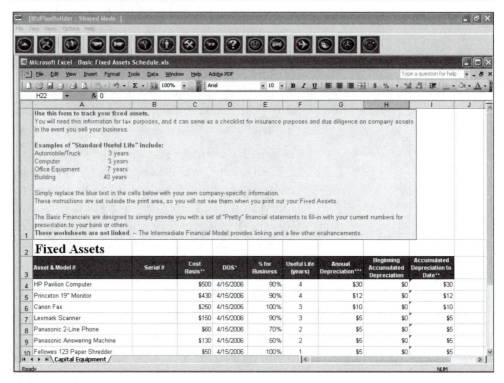

Current Assets   These are cash and other assets that are expected to be turned into cash or consumed within one year. These include investments; accounts receivable and notes; inventory (including raw materials, work in process and finished goods); and other current assets. Other current assets include prepaid expenses, such as insurance premiums or advertising costs that must be paid in advance but are "used up" over a period of time.

Fixed Assets   These are assets (also called Plant and Equipment) that are of a durable nature and are expected to help generate revenue over a period of a year or longer. Fixed assets can include equipment, vehicles, furniture and fixtures, land, and buildings. They are listed at cost on the balance sheet and are depreciated over a period of years. Depreciation is recorded as an expense in the budget, and to an account called accumulated depreciation on the balance sheet, which acts as a reduction to the total value of the fixed assets.

Other Assets   This asset category may include such accounts as patents, copyrights, or goodwill.

On the other side of the balance sheet are liabilities and equity.

Liabilities

Liabilities are those accounts or debts that your business owes others, and they are commonly grouped into Current Liabilities and Long Term Debt.

Current Liabilities   These are debts that are expected to be repaid within a year, including short term debt payable to the bank (including the portion of long-term debt due within one year); accounts payable to suppliers for materials, supplies, and the like; other payables for items like payroll taxes or sales taxes; and accrued liabilities (such as bonuses or pension plans that are paid in the future but relate to performance over the current or prior fiscal period).

Long-Term Debts   These are those loans from a bank or other lenders that are due to be repaid over a period of a year or longer. Usually, these loans are mortgages or were used to purchase fixed assets.

Equity

The final category on the balance sheet is equity. Although the exact listing of accounts is determined by what type of business you own (i.e., a proprietorship, partnership, or corporation), the equity category summarizes the accumulated wealth of your company. This includes capital, which is the amount that has been invested into your company, retained earnings, which are the accumulated profits (or losses) the company has earned from operations less dividends declared, and dividends payable, which are dividends that have been declared but not yet paid to the shareholders. Equity is the value that is left after you've subtracted your total liabilities from your total assets.

Beginning Balance Sheet Balances

As soon as you spend or invest your first dollar, you have a financial position that can be presented on a balance sheet. The equity section would reflect your personal investment, as well as any money invested from other sources. Assets may have been purchased, liabilities may have been incurred, and expenses have probably been incurred.

Because a balance sheet reflects your cumulative financial position through a certain day, all activity that occurs prior to your first budget month must be added to the new activity for that month to accurately project your balance sheet as of the end of the first budget month. Therefore, you (and your accountant in the case of large ventures) will need to calculate what your beginning balance sheet balances are—what your balance sheet would show on the day before you start your budget period—so that these beginning balance sheet amounts can be incorporated into your projections.

■ Projecting Financial Statements—That Support Your Assumptions

Whether you are researching a business proposal, starting a new business, or expanding an existing business, there are two main reasons why you want to prepare projected financial statements. The first is to determine if your proposed business venture, expansion, or project can be successful, and the second is to set goals and to chart a financial course for your business to follow in the future.

For either purpose, you will need to research the probable expenses of the venture and the market sales potential, and then quantify the results of this research in your projected financial statements.

Be Conservative

When projecting your financial statements, you should follow the accounting principle of conservatism. Conservatism states that if there is a choice of values, the more conservative value must be chosen: the lower value for an asset or revenue item, the higher value for an expense or debt. One of the first things potential lenders or investors will be looking at is reasonableness. In other words, are the numbers you've projected possible? Lenders and investors may form an impression of you as an individual based on how reasonable they think your projected financial statements are. If they get the impression that you're the type of person who embellishes a lot, they may begin to question all of your financial projections, as well as other parts of your business plan.

Remember, projected financial statements do not stand on their own. They must be supported by research on your market that indicates your business or venture can be successful. Do not manipulate the numbers in your projected financial statements to indicate the possibility of success if the research in your written business plan does not support those numbers!

Consider Multiple Projection Scenarios

You may want to prepare not only one set of projections, but three—that is, generating three sets of BizPlanBuilder financials. They should include a pessimistic (worst case) scenario, an optimistic (best case) scenario and a realistic (most likely) scenario. In this way, you will have a true picture of your potential for gain and loss. While the best case is what you hope for, the worst case is what you need to be prepared for; in the meantime, the most likely case will be the basis for many of your decisions. These scenarios would then be presented in a narrative form in your Financial Plan (or Considerations).

How Much Money Do I Need?

In order to estimate your capital requirements, you will need to consider each of the potential uses for the financing funds, including (but not limited to): research and development, fixed asset purchases and working capital. As you analyze each, you'll need to project how much money you'll need, when you'll need it, and what type of financing is most appropriate for each.

Financing Research and Development

You may need funds to finance R&D activities in order to turn a product concept into a prototype, and a prototype into a final product. Frequently, there is a long delay between the time money is paid out for research and development expenses and the time sales and profits are generated as a result of the efforts. Because of this, it may be appropriate to fund your R&D activities with long-term financing.

The Comprehensive Financial Model in BizPlanBuilder includes a worksheet specifically designed for projecting R&D. Here the R&D budget can be estimated and reveal the entire projection over the next five years. As your business builds, you can enter actual numbers in the prior years' R&D Investment schedule and use this data to refine future budget projections.

Financing Fixed Asset Purchases

You may need funds to finance fixed asset purchases such as new equipment to produce a new product or a larger manufacturing facility to increase your production capacity. As for R&D expenses, there is often a long delay between the time money is paid out for fixed assets purchases and the time sales and profits are generated as a result of the new assets. Also, the dollar values of fixed asset purchases can be very large. For these reasons, fixed asset purchases are almost always funded with long term-financing.

Financing Working Capital

Working capital is the cash that allows a business to operate, stock inventory, and carry accounts receivable before collecting the money from customers. The financing requirement for working capital is "permanent" and grows proportionally with growth in sales volume. Growth consumes a lot of cash. Many people overlook the fact that if your sales increase 50%, your working capital requirements may also increase about 50%. In other words, if you have $200,000 in working capital and sales increase 50%, you may need an additional $100,000 in working capital. Frequently, short-term debt can be arranged using your accounts receivable and inventory as collateral. However, this is not always the best approach. If you repeatedly need to borrow money to fund working capital, it may be more appropriate to obtain long-term financing, if possible.

Your cash flow statement can assist you in determining how much money you need by anticipating your actual cash requirements. Once you've projected how much money you think you will need to finance each of these areas, incorporate them into your cash flows statements in the appropriate time periods. Then review your cash flows statements and look for large cash balances or shortfalls indicated by the numbers in parentheses; you may need to adjust the amounts of your financing requirements or the timing of those requirements.

Once you've refined your financing projections, add the amounts you've projected for each financing use, then estimate an additional percentage over that sum to use as your total financing requirement; a general guideline to follow is to raise 50% more capital than your projections indicate you'll need. The Comprehensive Financial Model has worksheet for Capital Requirements that automatically flow into appropriate sections in the assumptions worksheets and will be included on your financial statements.

▶ **Do It in BizPlanBuilder**

The Comprehensive Model's Cash Flow worksheets are partly filled in by other worksheets automatically. This loss is reported from the Budget sheet:

■ Using the Financial Plan Spreadsheets

The spreadsheets Masters included in BizPlanBuilder are standard spreadsheet template files that have been modified to substantiate the financial projections and requirements of your business plan. Within these spreadsheets, generic financial statements/analyses have been constructed using labels and formulas in many of the spreadsheet cells; other cells are formatted to accept the values you enter. In addition to empty cells in which you enter data, there is placeholder text for information you must enter that is formatted in a blue font.

These generic financial statements provide the structure for presenting a professional level of financial detail using standard accounting formats and terms. By providing this structure, the BizPlanBuilder spreadsheet templates can help simplify the task of projecting financial statements for your business.

The particular set of financial statements you need will vary depending on the nature of your business and your purpose for writing a business plan. The **Basic Financial Statements** is a group of separate spreadsheet templates suitable for service and product ventures that includes a basic balance sheet, cash flow projection, fixed assets (such as your office computer equipment and the like), income statement for profit and loss, even startup cash spreadsheet, invoice log, and services list designed for service business plans and, when edited, a bank loan plan for virtually any kind of small or home office-type business.

The **Intermediate Financial Model** is actually a series of integrated worksheets contained in one Excel workbook. This model is designed for the prospective business owner or entrepreneur to easily determine the financial feasibility of a new venture. (Its templates can also be used as a planning tool for an ongoing business.) The spreadsheets contained in Intermediate Financial Model workbook include basic assumptions, fixed assets, income statement, balance sheet, and cash flow.

The **Comprehensive Financial Model** is also a series of worksheets in one Excel workbook. This financial model is designed for the same purpose as the Intermediate Financial Model. However, there is more detailed in the comprehensive version. The workbook itself contains what may look like an overwhelming amount of detail and documentation to the new business entrepreneur or student. Such an eye-opener will show you the kind of number-crunching that can be necessary as well as intricately automated—just like income tax software.

Historical Financials	Gross Profit - Years 2–3
Assumptions-Human Resources	Gross Profit - Years 1–5
Human Resources Plan	Budget - Year 1
Capital Requirements	Budget - Years 2–3
Revenue Model	Budget - Years 1–5
Assumptions - Sales	Income - Year 1
Assumptions - Cost of Goods Sold	Income - Years 2–3
Assumptions - Marketing	Income - Years 1–5
Assumptions - Research & Development	Balance - Year 1
Assumptions - General & Administrative Expense	Balance - Years 2–3
	Balance - Years 1–5
Assumptions - Other	Cash Flow - Year 1
Assumptions - Balance Sheet	Cash Flow - Years 2–3
Gross Profit - Year 1	Cash Flow - Years 1–5
	Ratios

Break-Even	Valuation Summary
Ratio Analysis	Capitalization Table
Sensitivity Analysis	Investor Analysis

A typical Service plan, however, may only feature a budget, balance sheet, and projected income statement. Additionally, cash flows statements (also known as statements of changes in financial position) and analyses such as gross profit and break-even may also be included. In all likelihood, you will have to carefully "tweak" and edit the content of the model you use—basic, intermediate, and comprehensive—while respecting the formulas and integration of the Excel templates and with the advice of your accountant or financial adviser.

Consult the special instructions provided in BizPlanBuilder's predesigned and preformatted Excel workbooks and worksheets. These instructions appear in green text at the beginning of each worksheet where applicable.

Getting Started with the Spreadsheets

Follow these general steps to complete your financial statements:

1. Locate the spreadsheet files templates in BizPlanBuilder.

2. Right-click the template(s) and select **Add to Current Plan**.

3. Then open the spreadsheet file you want to use in your current plan.

4. Click **OK** to close the BizPlanBuilder warning window (shown below) that advises you how to properly save your work.

5. **Enter your values into the spreadsheet(s).** Enter your estimated values into each spreadsheet you need. Replace the sample values with your values.

    Wherever the text is blue you can overwrite what is in that cell. Of course, you may notice a formula in a cell with blue text.

In this detail (below) from the Cash Flow Projection spreadsheet in the Basic Financial Statements, the selected cell is blue, a value you replace with your data.

4	Cash Flow Projection	Jan
5		
6	Cash Beginning	$0 ← Selected cell
7	Cash Receipts	$0
8	Cash Disbursements	$0

6. **Recalculate the spreadsheet(s).** When you have finished entering your estimated values, be sure each spreadsheet recalculates.

    After the spreadsheet is recalculated, some cells may display **********. This indicates that the value in the cell is too large for the column width. Set the column width to at least five characters more than the number of digits in the value (this allows for dollar signs, commas and parentheses). For example, to display ten million dollars (which has eight digits), your column width should be at least 13.

7. Review your financial statements. Review the financial statements, either on screen or by printing drafts. Your projections should be conservative and realistic, and you should have assumed sufficient financing to maintain a positive cash balance. Refine your financial statements as needed.

8. Print your completed financial statements for review if desired before compiling your business plan.

9. **Summarize your financial projections.** Analyze your completed financial statements. Summarize your financial projections in the Financial Plan document template (see Financial Plan Narrative Text).

■ BizPlanBuildercise 4.1: Adding a Financial Plan Template

> **Now that you are familiar with launching BizPlanBuilder 10, steps will be further streamlined for opening the BizPlanBuilder window and adjusting your workspace.**

1. Launch BizPlanBuilder and choose to work on the LogaTorial business plan used in the previous exercises—or use your own plan.

2. In the Item List of the BizPlanBuilder window, locate the Financial Model – Intermediate. If necessary, expand the file tree to reveal the intermediate financial model workbook icon.

3. Right-click [Financial Model - Intermediate].

4. Select **Add to Current Plan** from the shortcut menu.

5. BizPlanBuilder adds a copy of the template to your plan and appears at the bottom of the list.

> **When you add spreadsheets to your business plan, they are not part of the final assembled plan. You can print them separately and place them after the Financial Models introduction page.**

6. Close BizPlanBuilder if desired or leave open for next exercise.

■ Printing the Financial Statements

The Intermediate and Comprehensive Financial Model workbooks feature ActiveX controls for quick printouts of worksheets, such as a Cash Flow sheet [Print CF] and entire workbooks [Print Financials]. Simply click on the desired printout button and the print job will automatically be sent to your default printer. For the Excel worksheets in the Basic Financial Plan template, you can print all or part of your financial spreadsheets from within the BizPlanBuilder program using Excel's print features and your specific printer. (You can also use these same features for printing spreadsheets in the Intermediate and Comprehensive financial models, too.) The following are a few general guidelines that may assist you with printing the BizPlanBuilder financial statements.

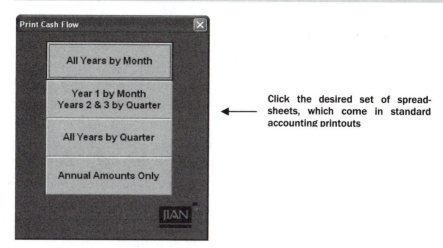

Print options for the Cash Flow statement in the Intermediate financial model.

Click the desired set of spread-sheets, which come in standard accounting printouts

1. **Save the spreadsheet before issuing a print command.** This protects your work in the event that your system locks up while attempting to execute the print command. Use the "Save As" command and give the spreadsheet a new name. That way you'll still have the original document as well.

2. **Set the printer/page setup options for the spreadsheet or range.** For example, you may want to print a landscape-oriented Cash Flows Statement on letter-size paper with a portrait (vertical) orientation and a standard font size, since the statement is only six columns wide. Though the default settings for even the Basic Financial Statements templates are usually adequate, you can set your printer/page setup options to best fit your needs or the requirements of your printer.

3. **Print the spreadsheet or selected range.**

4. **Repeat these steps for each statement you want to print.**

■ BizPlanBuildercise 4.2: Open and Print the Cash Flow Statement

1. Launch BizPlanBuilder if necessary and choose to work on the LogaTorial business plan used in previous exercises—or use your own plan.

2. In the BizPlanBuilder window, locate the Financial Model – Intermediate in the current plan portion of the left pane.

3. Double-click the **Financial Model – Intermediate** icon.

4. Use the navigation buttons in bottom-left corner of the Excel window to scroll to the Cash Flow worksheet.

5. Click **Print CF**.

The Print CF dialog box appears.

6. Click the **Year 1 by Month Years 2 & 3 by Quarter**.

7. If your printer is configured correctly, BizPlanBuilder will automatically print the Cash Flow worksheet.

8. Close BizPlanBuilder if desired or leave open for next exercise.

Customizing the Financial Statements

BizPlanBuilder spreadsheets can help simplify the task of projecting financial statements for your business. The generic financial statements provide a professional level of financial detail using standard accounting formats and terms.

Although the spreadsheets were designed to meet the needs of a variety of businesses, there will be situations that require customization of some of the financial statements. While the publisher, author, and the makers of BizPlan-Builder cannot be held responsible for the integrity of any customized spreadsheets, there are some guidelines to help you successfully customize the spreadsheet to meet your needs. These guidelines address the common customization needs of previous BizPlanBuilder users.

In this discussion, "customizations" refers to overwriting labels and formulas in locked (protected) cells, not to inputting sales item labels or estimated values in the provided cells. Do not attempt to customize the BizPlanBuilder spreadsheets unless you are an experienced Excel user! You can irreparably damage the integrity of the spreadsheets by editing or deleting certain cells. Such changes also cause a ripple effect because many of the functions in spreadsheet cells depend on the integrity of other worksheets in the workbook.

General Customization Guidelines

The BizPlanBuilder spreadsheets are delivered with some cells formatted as locked (protected), and with protection enabled for the spreadsheet itself. This was done to prevent formulas and important labels from being overwritten by accident, which could irreparably damage the integrity of the spreadsheet.

It is important to know this before you begin entering data—and for customizing your financials. If you try to edit a locked cell when protection is enabled for the Excel workbook file, Excel will disallow the edit and give you a message that the cell is locked (protected). Therefore, you may need to disable the protection for the spreadsheet file before you can perform any customizations. This is done by right-clicking the protected cell, clicking the **Protection** tab of the Format Cells dialog box, and deselecting ☑ Locked .

For other issues that you encounter when customizing workbook templates, refer to Excel's Help feature—and follow these general guidelines as well.

1. **Save your Excel workbook file twice before you begin any customization work.** To minimize the customizations you'll need to make, be sure you've entered your assumptions or estimated values and fine-tuned them as needed until the calculated results are as close as possible to an accurate projection of your business's position. Then, save the workbook under a different file name as a backup in case you change your mind or make an error.

    To do this in BizPlanBuilder, perform a **File>Save As** procedure in the Excel window and save the workbook with a slightly altered filename (e.g., "Financial Model--Intermediate**2**). Then close the workbook in BizPlan-Builder and reopen the original again in BizPlanBuilder.

To replace your original workbook with a backup, navigate in Windows Explorer to where the workbook is saved. By default, it is in a subfolder in the username subfolder, which is in the **BusinessPlan** folder on your desktop by default. Delete the original workbook (e.g., Financial Model--Intermediate) and rename the backup (e.g., Financial Model--Intermediate2) to the original's filename (e.g., Financial Model--Intermediate).

If you choose to work on financials that have been incorporated into the current plan, you will need to use the Windows Explorer method to rename the plan to correspond to the file name in the Current Plan pane.

2. **Unprotect the Excel file.** This is done by clicking **Tools, Protection,** and then **Unprotect Sheet**. For workbooks that contain more than one sheet, you may need to unprotect additional sheets. Protected cells require a different procedure for unlocking them.

3. **Make your customizations.** In general, the BizPlanBuilder workbook templates are designed so that changes to a cell affect cells to the right of and below the changed cell; cells to the left of and above a changed cell are usually not affected. Because of this structure, it is best to work on one row at a time across (left to right) and down in the spreadsheet.

4. **Refer to How Do I . . .? for specific guidelines.** The How Do I . . .? section that follows this list provides suggestions on making customizations for several specific situations. Check this section to see if your situation (or one close to it) is discussed.

5. **Reprotect the spreadsheet file.** Once you've completed your customizations, we strongly recommend that you reprotect the spreadsheet file so cells cannot be overwritten by accident. This is done by clicking **Tools, Protection,** and then **Protect Sheet**.

6. **Review the spreadsheet, and resave the file.** Recalculate the spreadsheet file, then scroll through it and review the results of your customizations. Make sure that an error condition has not been created as a result of a change you made, and "manually" spot-check a few of the totals to ensure the logic of the formulas is still intact. If everything appears correct, resave the spreadsheet file. It is strongly recommend that you keep the backup file (the one you saved under a different filename before you made the customizations) in case you discover an error later on. This can help you avoid "starting over from scratch."

How Do I . . .?

All of BizPlanBuilder's financials templates have instructions and tips for entering data and making certain kinds customizations. Wherever the text is blue, you can overwrite what is in that cell. You will want to change the placeholder text, for example, to accurately describe the depreciable items that your business uses. You will also notice that formulas can appear in cells in a blue font. For example, in the Intermediate Balance Sheet you will notice that many of the cells with Blue text reference the previous cell. Instead of overwriting the cell, one method of modification would be to press F2 then type a plus (+) or minus (-) sign, then the adjustment for that period, and press Enter.

When applicable:

- Complete all of the appropriate blue text areas on the Basic Assumptions sheet.

- Do not forget to select how your dollars are entered:
  - Whole dollars
  - Thousands, or
  - Millions

- Be consistent in the way you enter your data.

The following are tips for handling some of the other customization issues previous *BizPlanBuilder® Express* users have encountered.

How do I rename a Budget-type expense items?

You may want to rename one or more of the expense items on one of the budget-type worksheets (e.g., Assumptions-Marketing in the Comprehensive financial model) that you don't need in order to "add" item(s) that you do need (or to clarify the name of an item).

To rename an investment/expense item, locate the row for the item in the applicable worksheet, then replace the sample name by entering the name you want. Make sure that the "new" item does not repeat another category as the item you are replacing.

If the workbook is integrated, the new name should "flow" into the appropriate cells.

How do I add rows for more items?

You may want to add one or more rows to accommodate additional item(s). If so, you can customize the Excel worksheet to add rows directly to the desired spreadsheet statement. **However, adding rows can jeopardize the integrity of the spreadsheet and the accuracy of the financial statements.** For this reason, it is strongly recommended that you consider renaming items instead (as discussed above), and/or consolidating values for several related items to use only one row. BizPlanBuilder's templates usually supply extra rows to the categories that may require them.

For the Intermediate and Comprehensive Financial Models, be very careful if you need to add a row given the high level of integration in these workbooks. In cases where integration is a factor, a new row will not flow into their predesigned worksheets. (If a higher level of customization is needed, expert Excel skills will be necessary to meet such a challenge.) Some of the Basic Financial Plan template worksheets are easier for this type of customization. However, the predesigned nature of even these worksheets warrants replacement of preexisting elements with new labels, placeholders, and other kinds of data.

How do I delete rows for unused items?

You may want to delete the rows that contain items that don't apply to your circumstances such as unused sales items, expense items, or balance sheet items. Before you make decisions on which rows to omit from your print-outs, keep in mind that including an item with zero values lets anyone who reviews your business plan know that you considered the item and deliberately set it to zero. A "missing" item may cause a reviewer to think you overlooked the item. This is especially true for expense, cash flow and balance sheet items.

Make sure that the row you are deleting is not a totaling row. (Once you've deleted a row, you should verify that the total for that category is still being calculated correctly.) Also, if the item you deleted appears on another worksheet in an integrated financials workbook, you will want to delete it from the other worksheet as well for consistency. Make sure you review every affected worksheet to check the impact of your deleted row. If deletion is not a viable option, you should indicate unused rows with N/A for not applicable.

■ Financial Plan Checklist

√ Have you secured the advice of your accountant and/or financial advisor? (This check relates to all that follow, for you will need the input of these professionals if you or they prepare your spreadsheets.)

√ Have you done the background research necessary to prepare your financial statements: operating expenses, sales projections, etc.?

√ Have you prepared three sets of financial projections (best case, worst case, most likely case)?

√ Have you completed the appropriate projected financial statement worksheets for your business?

√ Have you carefully analyzed each financial statement, and do you understand the significance of the numbers you're projecting?

√ Do you know how much capital you need and when you need it? Have you determined what types of financing are appropriate?

√ Can you explain in detail how you plan to use any financing you receive?

√ Have you summarized your financial position in a written Financial Plan, which is part of your business plan?

√ Have you consulted a business analyst for assistance when needed?

√ Have you included projected and historical financial statements in either the Financial Model or the Supporting Documents section of your plan?

√ Have you determined an exit/payback strategy for lenders and investors?

■ Review Questions 4.1

1. What is meant by "pro forma" financial statements?

   _____

   _____

   _____

2. Why would you want to include a Personal Financial Statement spreadsheet or table in your business plan?

   _____

   _____

   _____

   _____

3. What is the income statement? How does it differ from the budget statement?

   _____

   _____

   _____

   _____

4. What is the balance sheet?

   _____

   _____

   _____

5. When should you conduct a break-even analysis? What does the contribution margin represent? Which BizPlanBuilder financial model provides this analysis?

   _____

   _____

   _____

   _____

6. Why should you follow the principle of conservatism when projecting your financial statements?

_____

_____

_____

7. Common to all three BizPlanBuilder financial plan templates is the cash flow projection. What is it and how is it used?

_____

_____

_____

_____

8. What is working capital? Why is it so critical to the health of your business? Which BizPlanBuilder financial model and worksheet would you use to project this?

_____

_____

_____

_____

9. What is the purpose of the small red triangles in the cells of BizPlanBuilder Excel worksheets?

_____

_____

_____

10. Where can you enter data in BizPlanBuilder template worksheets? Why is it important to leave cells protected?

_____

_____

_____

_____

■ Activities 4.1

To familiarize yourself with a BizPlanBuilder Excel template and the concepts introduced in Part 4, perform the following activities.

1. a. Imagine that you are caterer Chris Jordan and you are projecting the first two years of business for PartyWorks, from which you will make decisions about your profitability and the size of your loan.

   b. Using the following data, select the correct BizPlanBuilder template from the Basic Financial Statements and enter the data:

Information is per year:	2006	2007
Salaries and Wages	$49,000.00	$59,500.00
Credit Card & Bank Charges	$17,900.00	$18,100.00
Equipment Rental and Leases	$9,000.00	$10,000.00
Beer, Wine, & Liquor	$25,000.00	$29,000.00
Food Supplies	$30,500.00	$42,000.00
Utilities	$5,500.00	$6,500.00
Insurance (Liability, etc.)	$11,000.00	$12,300.00
Property Insurance	$3900.00	$3,900.00
Taxes, Licenses, & Fees	$12,000.00	$12,000.00
Van (purchase and fuel)	$24,000.00	$700
Revenue from services	$137,800.00	$230,300.00

In addition to the above data, Chris has to pay $49,000 per year to service the loan that he foresees is needed. The projected revenue for both years is an assumption.

2. What are the total operating expenses for the first year?

   _____

3. What are the total operating expenses for the second year?

   _____

4. Will Chris have a negative or positive net income? If not, what might he do to change this scenario?

   _____

   _____

5. What might Chris do to edit this Excel sheet to make it look neater?

   _____

   _____

■ Financial Plan Narrative Text

The written Financial Plan portion of your business plan should be composed of brief and direct explanatory paragraphs—and they should summarize your financial position. This is where you "go for the close," summarizing your business plan presentation and asking for the cash.

The Service/Bank Loan Financial Plan requires judicious editing, much of it informed by the real numbers generated by the financial model spreadsheets.

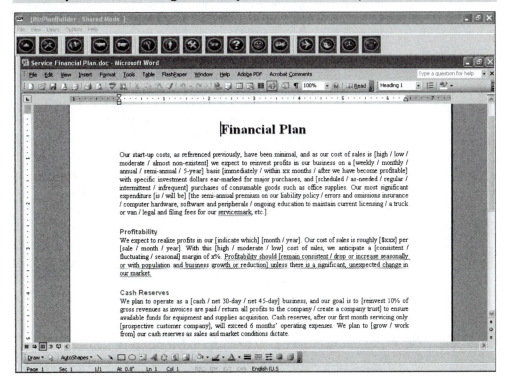

The financial plan does not include your projected financial statements, historical financial statements (if applicable), or financial analyses. These should be included with other relevant information in the Financial Models and/or Supporting Documents section of your business plan. Exactly what you say in your Financial Plan is dependent on your type of business, your target audience for your business plan and your purpose for writing a business plan.

Keep in mind that projected financial statements do not stand on their own. Anyone reviewing your financial statements will also expect to read a discussion that supports the projections you made (research on market, competition, and the like). If you are using your business plan to apply for a loan or solicit investors, you need to target your statements to the interests and concerns of your potential lenders and investors. The basic question to ask yourself when writing the Financial Plan section of your business plan is: "What would I want to know to evaluate a business proposal before I would consider investing my own money?"

The financial plan overview at the beginning of Part 4 has some information that can give you some perspective on what lenders and investors will be looking for in your business plan. Again, consult your accountant and financial advisor if you need additional assistance to complete your Financial Plan narrative.

You may also need to expand your narrative with additional BizPlanBuilder template templates.

The **Capital Requirements** template in the Angel/VC, Internet, and Retail plans may be required to describe the operating requirements for the years projected in the financial statements. This operating working capital is defined as the cash in the bank, the accounts receivable, and the inventory the accounts payable. In the Comprehensive Financial Model this is calculated from the values on the Balance Sheet for years 1–5. This same component is where you also discuss the level of safety for a business loan or investment—and the "Use of Proceeds," that is, specifically how the loan and or line of credit funds are to be used.

The other template that supplements the Financial Plan is the **Exit/Payback Strategy**. Financial projections should show how loan and investment funds help generate the profits and cash required for payback and exit. Here you can discuss increases in profits and cash flows that (1) result from financing and (2) are earmarked to pay back the loans and investors. The narrative must explain how much time will be required before the loan is paid back (or when investors can exit, that is, when they can convert their equity. More people are now going into business actually anticipating their exit—or "harvest"—strategy. If you are successful, even moderately successful, "selling out" might be the best way to get ROI for yourself and investors—and many investors expect to see how you intend to do this with an Initial Public Offering (IPO).

■ BizPlanBuildercise 4.3: Review the Financial Plan

In this exercise you will open and review your Financial Plan template.

1. In BizPlanBuilder and open your Financial Plan template.

2. Review the wording of each section and any Expert Comments in the document. If you are using the Service/Bank Loan Plan, temporarily add the Financial Template from the Angel/VC master to complete the next steps.

3. Scroll to the following Expert Comment:

> ❖ Valuation: Valuation is very important, but don't obsess over it, or be penny-wise and pound-foolish. You must give credit to the value added by your angel or venture investors. Everyone gets a piece of a much larger pie than you would without your investor's money and experience.

4. Note the "philosophical" approach you should take as much as being utterly accurate you must be in interpreting your spreadsheet data. The key idea is "You must give credit to the value added by your angel or venture investors."

5. Continue scrolling through the document, reviewing the Assumptions section and the tables at the beginning of the Financial Statements section.

6. Note that the Financial Statements is headed by two kinds of tables. Only one is used. The first is a standard Word table, in which you can insert data.

The other table is a convenient embedded Excel table object, which has formulas to generate the projections.

7. For income ratios, there is also a Word table and a convenient link to the BizStats.com site (**http://www.BizStats.com/**). There you can retrieve data for your industry.

   BizStats.com. This online statistics engine can show you what the average small business owner keeps from each dollar of revenue. It can then be compared to an industry profitability summary for sole proprietorships. Other kinds and sizes of business can also be compared for the purpose of preparing a business plan and its financials. Retail stats are given for sales per square foot, sales per store, and so on. Other metrics include safe and risky small business startups and success ratios.

8. Scroll down in the Financial Plan template document and review the narrative sections for Gross Profit Analysis, Budget, Income Statements, Balance Sheet, Break-Even Analysis, and Cash Flow Statements.

9. As you can see, the order of the narrative follows the order of the worksheets in the Comprehensive Financial Models. If your business plan utilizes the Intermediate Financial Model, certain sections can be omitted, such as the Budget and the Break-Even Analysis.

   How would you adapt a template to fit your needs?

   _____

   _____

   _____

10. Close the Financial Plan and BizPlanBuilder if desired.

He that wants money, means, and content is without three good friends.
—*William Shakespeare*

I like putting things together, and seeing how they work.
—*Nicholas Cage*

Part 5: Assembling Your Business Plan

Part 5 of *BizPlanBuilder Express* shows you how to assemble your plan in Biz-PlanBuilder and surveys the document templates that help with plan presentation and funding. (The appendix covers templates for preplanning and managing your business once it is in operation.)

There are three main sections in Part 5:

- **Assembling the Business Plan in BizPlanBuilder** takes you through the step-by-step the process of launching the Assemble Plan Preview utility.

- **Using Supporting Documents**—`Supporting Documents`—reviews selected supporting document resources that you can use to substantiate your business plan such as press releases, resumes of key individuals, core values statements, and the like. (You can also add documents from outside of the BizPlanBuilder Item List.)

- In addition to the supporting documents, the `Plan Presentation` and templates will also be surveyed in this section.

- **Funding Your Plan** details dozens of different methods and sources for securing funding—and surveys how this topic is also covered in the `Resources` documents of the BizPlanBuilder program.

▶ **Learning Objectives**

After Completing Part 5, you should be able to:

1. Assemble and preview a business plan using BizPlanBuilder
2. Ensure your business plan has a professional appearance
3. Access and select from a list of additional documents that you can include to substantiate your business plan
4. Describe the purpose of various items that may be included with the business plan, such as Plan Presentation templates that include cover letter, nondisclosure agreement, and the clause that prohibits copying or further distribution
5. Know where to locate the different supplementary document libraries in BizPlanBuilder
6. Recognize the different methods and sources for securing financing, and determine which ones are appropriate for your business situation

■ Assembling and Previewing a Plan

Before you actually assemble a business plan in BizPlanBuilder, you should first review and "preflight" the plan. This is called Quality Assurance in many industries—and it applies to a good business plan, too. Achieving QA will not only ensure that your documents successfully communicate your business venture to the most critical readers, it will also give them an idea of the "tight ship" you intend to operate with your own and your lenders' investment.

Because the target audience will judge your business venture by the presentation of your plan, it should be clearly and concisely written, informative, and verifiable. Your plan must be presented and packaged in an effective and professional manner. This section covers many useful suggestions in these areas.

Reviewing Your Plan

As you by now know, your reader may only spend 5 to 10 minutes reviewing your business plan. The Executive Summary and Financials sections must encourage the reader to read the other sections of your business plan. Review the following questions with your plan in front of you either onscreen or in individual printouts. (Remember, in the BizPlanBuilder's Document pane, you have all the Microsoft Office editing and proofreading capabilities at your disposal.)

Does your plan address these important questions:

- Have I conveyed my company's vision?

- Do I have the management skills—or the team—in place?

- Is there a market for my service or product?

- Have I given a clear description of my product or service?

- Have I defined my target market?

- Do I understand my competitors' weaknesses and strengths?

- Are the Financials realistic and in line with lending patterns?

- Does the plan describe the ROI for the investor?

If your venture is well portrayed in your business plan, then distribute your plan for review and see what the reaction is.

You can, for example, use the Track Changes feature of Word to track your changes for review and revision. In the Microsoft Word document window, click the **Track Changes** button TRK in the Status Bar to turn this feature on and off. Then, you can e-mail the document for review to an associate or advisor. In the Microsoft Word menu bar, click **File**, **Send To**, and **Mail Recipient (for Review)** Mail Recipient (for Review)... to launch the Microsoft Outlook e-mail program.) When commented and revised documents are returned to you, you can open them in the Document pane of BizPlanBuilder and merge documents to revise any Word document in your business plan.)

If the plan passes this review and achieves your intended purpose immediately, congratulations!

You have now drafted a document that is easy and simple to update as needed. If revisions to your plan are recommended, and you agree with the recommendations, make the necessary changes in the BizPlanBuilder program and begin another cycle of QA. Some of the biggest success stories have come from people who received numerous rejections along the way. Use the recommendations to learn and apply what is necessary, and your next business plan will set you on the course to success.

"Preflighting" Your Plan

Your business plan may vary in length depending on the product or service and the intended purpose of the plan—as well as which BizPlanBuilder template you use and which components you decide to include. In most cases, limit the plan to anywhere from 5 to 35 pages, not including Financials and other supporting documents.

After you've completed the first draft of your business plan, be sure to check the plan for spelling, grammar and punctuation. You can use Word and Excel's powerful spelling and grammar checking features, of course. But always read word for word to make sure you have fully integrated your own text into the template and make sure that no stray placeholder text or punctuation is still left in your documents. You may want to solicit someone with editing skills to review the plan for both content and grammar. Errors can easily turn off a potential investor or other evaluator.

You can assemble as many preview versions of your plan as you want.

■ BizPlanBuildercise 5.1: Assemble and Save a Business Plan

By now it is assumed that you have performed at least some of the quality assurance tasks and are ready to assemble your business plan. If you do not have a business plan ready at this point, you can use the sample My Service Business Plan for LogaTorial for this hands-on exercise that explores the plan assembly process.

> **To prevent system hangs and for best results, exit out of any Microsoft Office program that is open, such as Word, Excel, and Outlook, before launching BizPlanBuilder and assembling a business plan.**

1. Launch BizPlanBuilder and select the LogaTorial or your business plan.

2. Click the checkbox after each document to include ☑ or exclude ☐ the documents you want assembled in the Current Plan area of the Item List.

3. Click **Assembly Plan Preview** button ⊗ in the BizPlanBuilder toolbar.

   OR

   In the BizPlanBuilder menu bar, click **File** and **Assembly Plan Preview**.

4. A message window appears informing you that open Word or Excel documents in BizPlanBuilder must be closed. Click **OK**.

   By default, the BizPlanBuilder Plan Assembly wizard saves your assembled plan as separate Word and Excel documents in a Business Plan folder on your desktop.

5. In the Save [Your Business Plan's Name] dialog box, click **Save** after you have accepted the defaults or changed the file location and name.

    The MIDAS program starts to assemble the plan. How long you wait depends on the length of the business plan, computer processor speed, and how much RAM your computer has. You will see the following progress window, which allows you to cancel the assembly process at any time.

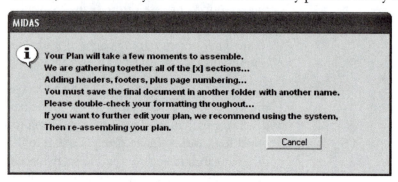

6. If MIDAS detects Excel worksheets in your plan assembly, the following dialog box appear.

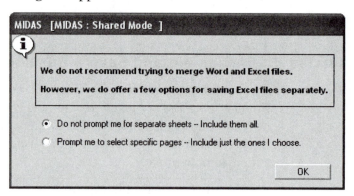

    Select from the following options:

    a. **Do not prompt me for separate sheets—Include them all**.

    OR

    b. **Prompt me to select specific pages—Include just the ones I choose**. If you choose this option, the Select the Excel Sheets to be Included dialog box, like the example shown on the next page, appears for each Excel worksheet in your business plan.

7. Click **OK**. The automated plan assembly process restarts.

    Depending on which option you selected in step 6, you may need to select options for several worksheets and click **OK** to proceed with the entire assembly. If not, you will only see the progress window.

8. When the MIDAS plan assembly wizard is finished, an information window opens informing you that the Word document—your plan's narrative—is open in BizPlanBuilder for review and further editing. To finish the assembly process, click **OK**.

Select the desired Excel worksheets for your financial plan. Hide the ones you do not need.

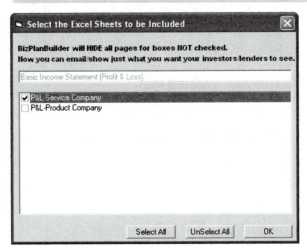

► **Do It in BizPlanBuilder**

After you assemble and save your business plan, it becomes possible to add Word formatting "globally" to all of the component parts of the finished plan. For example, you can add more information to the headers and footer, such as a date, descriptive running heads, and customized page numbering.

9. If you would like to review your plan without the Expert Comments, click the **Show/Hide Expert Comments** button on the BizPlanBuilder toolbar.

The assembled LogaTorial plan in the Document pane.

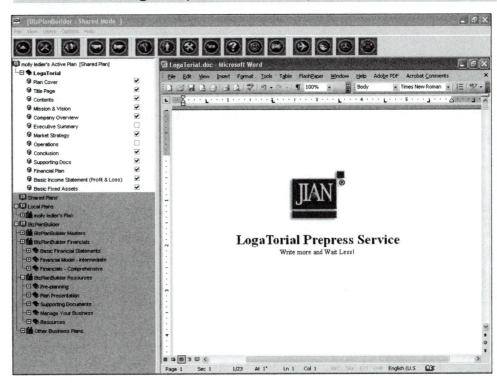

Reviewing Excel Documents in Your Assembled Plan

As you will readily see, when your assembled plan opens in Microsoft Word from within BizPlanBuilder, you can only view the Word documents of the plan narrative. To review the Excel documents, perform the following steps.

1. Click **File** in the BizPlanBuilder menu bar.

2. Click **View Excel Files of Assembled Plan**.

3. In the Select the Excel File to View dialog box, select the desired Excel file and click **OK.**

   Word closes in BizPlanBuilder and the selected Excel file opens.

Save the Assembled Plan

After reviewing and making any desired edits, save your plan:

1. Click **File** on the BizPlanBuilder menu bar.

2. Click **Save Assembled Plan As**.

3. In the Save As dialog box, navigate to the desired file location and enter a filename if necessary

4. Click **Save**.

5. Close BizPlanBuilder if desired.

■ Packaging Your Plan

Even if you are distributing your business plan as an e-mail attachment or as a Adobe Acrobat PDF document, make sure that you format it to look like a professional printed document. Many of the following suggestions and guidelines also apply.

Ideally, the final, distribution version of your plan should be printed on a quality laser or ink jet printer. For best results, make sure that the print quality is set for Best in your printer properties dialog box to achieve the best resolution, especially if you intend to make Xerox copies of your plan. Use high quality paper for the final copy. A 20-pound bond paper or better in white, ivory or gray creates a professional appearance.

If you want copies printed by a copy service such as Kinko's, you can create a high-resolution master copy or even provide the copy center with an electronic file of your plan, the spreadsheets, and any other related documents. Make sure that you properly collate your copies.

To ensure a professional appearance, limit your document to two or three fonts—which is ensured if you use the default BizPlanBuilder template formats. If you decide to custom format your plan, enhance the key points with bold, italic, or underline if desired. Standard, easily readable type, such as Arial for titles headings and Times New Roman for the body of the text, is recommended. The default template page setup is adequate for most plans. It frames your text by leaving a margin of about 1 inch around the top, bottom, left, and right margin. Don't be afraid to leave white space as this will make your plan easier to read—and make it easy for your readers to add their own notations.

The use of plastic spiral (GBC) binding or covers purchased at an office supply store will also provide a professional look. (This same service is provided by copy centers, too.) If your plan is going to bankers or investors, it helps if you can find a way to stand out from the crowd. Show some creativity by dressing up the cover to reflect something about your business.

Before distributing your business plan, have your lawyer, accountant and other professionals review and approve or sign off on the sections they helped prepare. You should number each plan and have a place for the signature of those to whom you are circulating the plan. This conveys the value of the plan and helps protect its proprietary nature. If appropriate, include a private placement disclaimer on the first sheet. It is also a good idea to include a personalized cover letter to each person to whom you send the plan, highlighting his or her particular interests.

■ Supporting Documents

Your supporting documents include information that supports the major points in the business plan—the items used to develop your plan. Include items that are too extensive to be included in the plan but assist the reader in understanding the plan's background and the rationale for your business and projections.

BizPlanBuilder's plan templates include a cover sheet `🗊 Supporting Documents` for this component of the business plan. Your may include some or all of the following documents:

- Articles of Incorporation and Corporate Bylaws (if applicable)

- Business and professional licenses, permits, and other legal documents

- Commitment letters from major customers, suppliers, and lenders

- Copies of contractual agreements

- Equipment in inventory

- Floor plan for retailer or manufacturer

- Letters of intent from suppliers, prospective customers, and so on.

- Market analysis data

- Organization chart and list of job responsibilities

- Patents (pending or issued), trademarks—or a letter from patent attorney stating likelihood of a patent being accepted

- Personal financial statements, tax returns, and credit reports of owners

- Price Schedule for product line or services

- Product specifications, photographs, brochures, drawings

- Proposed or executed lease or purchase agreement for building space and occupancy permits

- References (either letters or contact points) from lawyers, accountants, suppliers and banks

- Resumes of principals and other key people

- Samples of advertising copy or publicity articles

- Supplementary financial statements

- Tax and wholesale licenses

- Tax returns of principals for last three years

Adding External Documents

To add outside supporting documents to your business plan in BizPlanBuilder, they must be Microsoft Word documents, Excel workbooks, or PowerPoint presentations. They can be added to the current plan with the following steps:

1. Click **File** in BizPlanBuilder file menu

   OR

   Right-click inside the Current Plan area of the Item List.

2. Click **Add External Document**.

3. In the External Document dialog box, navigate to the desired document and click **Open**.

   The external document will be listed in the Current Plan area of the Item List. Word documents can be assembled directly into your plan. Excel and PowerPoint files are saved separately in your Business Plan folder.

BizPlanBuilder's Supporting Documents

The BizPlanBuilder Masters section of the Item List contains an expandable file tree of Supporting Document templates. For example, a template for the Personal Financial Statement is available patterned after the kind that banks use—and sometimes require for business loans. Other useful templates can help you develop your own core practices and core values.

Expanded Master Supporting Document file tree showing the available templates in BizPlanBuilder.

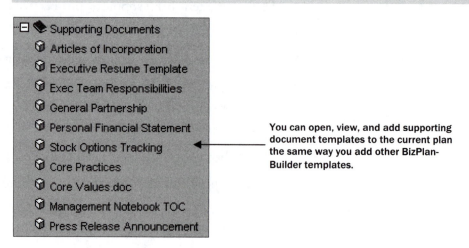

You can open, view, and add supporting document templates to the current plan the same way you add other BizPlan-Builder templates.

As with all important documents pertaining to your business, the documents that you include as supplementary information should not be originals. (Original documents should be stored in a secure place, such as a safety deposit box or a fire safe.) Because these documents can be sensitive in nature, consider including them with your business plan only upon request or if they are required. These should be only photocopies of the stored originals.

Given that the supporting documents are not included in the assembled plan's table of contents, you can list them in the Supporting Document cover page. Once your document is assembled, you can customize the table of contents if desired to add them there. You can also add page numbers in Word if desired and perform other kinds of customizations to further integrate external documents into your business plan to achieve the most professional appearance possible.

■ BizPlanBuildercise 5.2: Access and Examine a Supporting Document

In this exercise, you can examine one or more of the Supporting Document templates and sample documents.

1. Launch BizPlanBuilder if necessary and open the LogaTorial plan or your own business plan.

2. In the BizPlanBuilder Masters area of the Item List, scroll down to ◆ Supporting Documents and expand the file tree.

3. Right-click the ▯ Personal Financial Statement and select **Open**.

4. Click **OK**.

5. Expand the Document pane as desired.

6. Review the content of this Supporting Document template, including the Expert Comments.

7. Close the Personal Financial Statement and BizPlanBuilder if desired.

Optional Exercise. Open and review the Core Values and Core Practices supporting documents, which have standard boilerplate text that you can adapt for your own.

■ Distribution

Now that you have your business plan written, you are ready to print and distribute it. Limit access to those individuals who are either potential investors or who may have significant impact on your business.

For tracking, number the plans and list the name of the individuals who have received the copy. (You can add a placeholder for this number on the title page while in the Document pane—and before you assemble the plan.) Don't print and distribute a slew of copies. You are presenting your plan to a select audience. Only print and distribute a limited number of copies with that number printed in such a way to indicate your "limited edition"—for example, "Copy 3 of 12" or "Copy 3/12." If you release different versions of the document, you may want to add a code to the number such as "Copy 12C."

Prohibit copying by including a statement on the Title Page or Table of Contents, such as the verbiage provided by your Title Page template or edit to read as follows:

The contents of this plan are proprietary and confidential. It is not to be copied or duplicated in any way.

You should also appreciate that since your document is technically "published," it is also protected by U.S. Copyright Law.

It is important to place a disclaimer on your title page to indicate that your plan is not an offering for sale but rather a document for informational purposes. Consult an attorney for a recommendation on the appropriate disclaimer. An example of a typical disclaimer might is provided by the Title Page template:

This is a business plan. It does not imply an offering of Securities.

Mailing out unsolicited business plans violates securities laws when the plan contains language offering to sell stock in your company. The only exception to this rule would be Rule 504, Private Placements, which does permit general solicitations. Do not mail out unsolicited plans or advertise for investors unless you qualify for the Rule 504 exemption.

If you are not sure, take the precaution of establishing a business or personal relationship with a prospective investor before you send them anything. Offers to family, friends, and business associates are rarely considered solicitation. Consult with your attorney, if necessary, to make sure that you are in compliance with this legality and any others that may now apply.

Finally, insist that a **Non-Disclosure Agreement** (NDA) be signed by each reader. This is a simple statement in which readers agree to refrain from revealing the plan's contents or ideas to anyone else. A Non-Disclosure Agreement template is available in the Plan Presentation Masters discussed in the next section.

■ Making Your Presentation

If you are using your plan to raise capital, you may want to personally present it to bankers or investors. Many of the rules that apply to writing the narrative apply to presenting the business plan to readers—even a live audience.

Keep it short and to the point. Limit your presentation to half an hour or less. Like your written plan, the presentation should be concise and easy to understand. Extract the most important points (see the Executive Summary in Part 2) and run through them in an interesting and logical way. Don't be afraid to be enthusiastic about your product or service, but be realistic in your claims. Use visual aids. Using Microsoft PowerPoint slides or overheads with simple points or phrases helps to keep your audience focused. (BizPlanBuilder includes a PowerPoint template for this purpose, which is discussed in this section.)

Involve several members of your management team. For example, have your marketing executive speak for five minutes and then have your financial executive review the highlights of his or her area. This will give your audience exposure to your team.

If appropriate, demonstrate your product or service. Bring a sample, if possible. Generating enthusiasm and excitement for your product or service is the best way to gain the confidence of the banker or investor. Leave a written copy of your business plan so the banker or investor can review information that may not have been covered by your presentation.

Using BizPlanBuilder's Plan Presentation Masters

There is still important paperwork that should accompany your business plan. There are also other kinds of "live" presentation methods to consider.

BizPlanBuilder's Plan Presentation Masters [◆ Plan Presentation] provides important resources that you will need to present the plan. There are four kinds of cover letters designed for submitting your business plan to (1) a banker, (2) a leasing agent, (3) an angel investor, and (4) a venture capitalist. Similarly, there are boilerplate templates for nondisclosure agreements with a banker, investor, or leasing agent. Finally, the Plan Presentation Masters include useful documentation and instructions such as how to summarize a deal, craft an "elevator pitch," present your business in a quick e-mail, and so on.

Shown below, the expanded Plan Presentation Masters file tree.

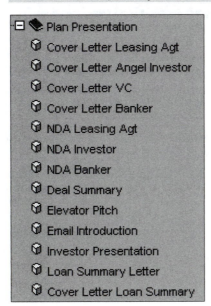

Cover Letter

When submitting a business plan, it is essential that you include a cover letter. The cover letter is the first document read, so keep it brief. At the same time, you want to motivate the reader to continue reading your business plan.

The cover letter should include name of your company and type of business; reason you have chosen this person to receive your plan; vision and mission of your company, in brief; intended purpose of submitting your business plan for evaluation; amount and type of funding you are seeking, if applicable; allocation/use of the funding, and return on investment for investor.

For example, in a cover letter to a banker, you are trying to establish a solid banking relationship that will help you deal with changes that occur to your venture's financial situation over time. Banks, being conservative, approach funding differently from other funding sources such as angel investors, venture capitalists, family, and friends. For lines of credit or loans, a bank needs to know how you made your business assumptions and created your business model. Your letter should show that you know what you will talk about with them and that you have the data to support your assumptions.

The Plan Presentation Masters template for this component also has useful information for what you should also get across to the bank. You need to establish that you have repaid loans in the past (a "track record") or that you have adequate collateral. And there are special inclusions for SBA lenders.[*]

Other cover letter templates may include Expert Comments specific to their content, as well. If they do not, read through them to familiarize yourself with the information you will need to customize them.

The closing paragraphs of the venture capitalist (VC) cover letter are designed for what is of interest to investors.

As LogaTorial Prepress Service's [xxx] solves the critical issue of [xxx] for [xx]% of customers, growth forecast at $[xx] million annually leads us to expect a significant increase in revenues by [Month / Quarter] of 20[xx]. We are on track for an [IPO / acquisition] by [month / quarter] of 20[xx].

A first-round investment of $[xxx] million will be used to [xxx], with planned second-round funding of $[xxx] million to complete [xxx] and market [xxx] in [xx] [type of market] markets.

The attached Executive Summary should answer most of your questions regarding this LogaTorial Prepress Service opportunity. We are prepared to make a full presentation, at your earliest convenience. LogaTorial Prepress Service must move swiftly to take advantage of the opportunity to [xxx]. I will call

early next week to arrange an appointment. Should you have questions in the meantime, please feel free to contact me on my cell phone at, [xxx-xxx-xxxx]. We look forward to meeting with you.

Best regards,

> It's important to include a telephone numbers where you can be reached. However, don't list more than two here, for it gives that, "fly-by-night" impression.

Molly LeDier
Founder & CEO
LogaTorial Prepress Service
(513) 555-8666
molly@logatorial.com

Even though the Plan Presentation masters provide you with boilerplate text, you should use company letterhead for any cover letter. After you finish composing your letter in BizPlanBuilder, you can easily cut and paste the letter text into your own cover letter template in Word—or any other word processor.

If you don't have company stationery, you can create a text-only letterhead from the Plan Presentation cover letter templates. Remember to include the proposed or existing company name, the address you are using for the business regardless if it is only temporary. You should also include any tele-

---

[*] The requirements for applications to the United States Small Business Administration change from time to time. For the most current information, visit the SBA Web site at: **www.SBA.gov**.

phone numbers for where you can be reached in addition to any telephone you include in the stationery's header or footer. (If you are working from home, it is highly recommended that you install a second line that is dedicated to calls to your business. This makes you look more professional and prevents giving businesspeople the wrong impression when, for example, a child answers the phone—often an embarrassing and uncomfortable experience for all parties.) These numbers can be placed at the end of your letter, in the "Please feel free to contact me" paragraph.

Finally, keep your cover letter to one page and remove any page number if one exists in the footer of the page.

Nondisclosure Agreement (NDA)

This agreement is designed to protect your company, ideas, assets and competitive position from inappropriate use of your confidential information by the evaluator of your business plan. Keep the agreement short, and make sure that it provides you with clear and adequate protection. Typically, the NDA is placed right after the cover letter. Most importantly, it should include language similar to the following, which is quoted in part from the BizPlanBuilder template for the nondisclosure agreement enclosed with a business plan submitted to a bank.

> It is acknowledged by Lender that information to be furnished is in all respects confidential in nature, other than information which is in the public domain through other means, and that any disclosure or use of same by Lender, except as provided in this agreement, may cause serious harm or damage to PartyWorks, Inc., and its owners and officers. Therefore, Lender agrees that Lender will not use the information furnished for any purpose other than as stated above, and agrees that Lender will not either directly or indirectly by agent, employee, or representative, disclose this information, [. . .]

The Plan Presentation Masters has three kinds of nondisclosure agreements for a banker, investor, or a lease agent. If you adapt one of these NDAs for kinds of evaluators who review the business plan, edit this agreement to fit the appropriate requirements. For this, you should always have the NDA reviewed by a qualified lawyer. The authors of this boilerplate, JIAN, cannot accept any liability for the legal effectiveness of this document. Also, do not submit electronic copies of the NDA in which the Expert Comments are still present in the document.

Other Plan Presentation Options

In addition to cover letter and NDA templates, the Plan Presentation Masters include other useful templates for managing the presentation of your plan:

- Deal Summary
- Elevator Pitch
- E-mail Introduction
- Investor Presentation

- Loan Summary Letter
- Cover Letter Loan Summary

The **Deal Summary** is an abstract of your business plan that contains all the crucial information about the business venture in a brief synopsis of each component in your business plan. This document, which can be from one to two pages, summarizes your investment opportunity in way that can be easily distributed by the primary reader to other interested parties in decision making that affects your plan.

The classic "**Elevator Pitch**" is the ability to describe your business venture succinctly in the course of an average elevator ride. It is based on the premise that you never know when you might find yourself standing next to the right person who can help you succeed in your business.

The template for this is actually a script designed to respond to such everyday questions as "What kind of work do you do?" or "How's business?" From these cues, you can tailor responses that will make people interested in your business. You never know, one of them might be your angel investor.

The **E-mail Introduction** is a simple message to friends, family, and other types of investors who would react positively to a less formal introduction to your business venture and its investment opportunities.

The **Investor Presentation** is a PowerPoint presentation template by BusinessPowerTools™. It is more of a tutorial and example. However, you can "Save as" this presentation and use copy from your finished plan to customize this PowerPoint slide presentation with the main points of your business plan.

The **Loan Summary** letter templates provide a summary letter in which you can list your funding and how much you are requesting from a loaner.

Another presentation template can be found in the Pre-Planning masters, which contains the **Investor Tracking** template. This is an Excel logbook for keeping track of investors and lenders who have a copy of your business plan. Use it to record your follow-up as well as readers' reactions.

▶ **Do It in BizPlanBuilder**

Click the BizPlanBuilder Workshop button 👆 on the toolbar to access business plan resources covering the topics discussed here from other viewpoints.

■ Following Up with Your Readers

After having completed and distributed the business plan, it is time to follow up with your potential investors and other readers. Approximately 7 to 10 days after you have delivered your business plan, follow up with a brief and professional phone call or letter to confirm that the evaluator has received your plan. Determine their reaction to your business plan and identify your next steps. See Funding Your Plan in this part of the book and Appendix B, Postplan Operations for additional resource materials.

■ Congratulations!

You now have an understanding of the process of creating business plan and how to use the computer application that makes that assists you in that process, BizPlanBuilder. You will spend much time and effort developing your business from a concept into something real. You will also spend a considerable amount of time going through the process of actually writing a business plan that you can assemble with BizPlanBuilder.

Your plan will not only communicate what your business is about, but will assist you in getting a better handle on your business and help build a foundation for business success. Congratulations on taking this first big step for your business and yourself.

■ Presenting Your Plan Checklist

√ Have you checked the spelling, grammar, and punctuation?

√ Has someone who has experience with other business plans or your business reviewed your plan?

√ Has your plan been reviewed by your financial and legal advisors?

√ Have you checked the plans formatting in Word (page numbers in the Table of Contents, footers, and any customizations added to the original template document)?

√ Have you taken steps to give your plan a professional appearance?

√ Have you printed the plan with a high-quality output printer?

√ Have you used 20-pound bond paper or better in white, ivory or gray?

√ Have you limited the plan to two or three typefaces? Arial for titles and Times New Roman or Palatino for the body of the text are recommended.

√ Have you enhanced key points with bold, italic or underline? Don't overdo the highlighting!

√ Have you left at least a one-inch margin at the top, bottom, and sides of the page?

√ Have you included index tabs to separate the sections of the plan?

√ Have you bound the business plan with GBC binding?

√ Have you numbered the title page of each copy?

√ Have your lawyer, accountant and other professionals reviewed and signed off on the sections they helped prepare?

√ Have you written a personalized cover letter to each person to whom you are sending the plan?

√ Have you included a nondisclosure agreement? If you're using the agreement that's in this book, has your attorney reviewed and approved it?

√ Have you reviewed your other presentation options?

■ Review Questions 5.1

1. Why should supporting documents, such as resumes of key personnel, be included with your business plan?

2. Why should someone other than you check the plan before printing—such as a legal or accounting professional?

3. Why should your business plan include a disclaimer that it is not implying an offering of securities?

4. What are some important points to keep in mind as you present your business plan?

5. What is a Non-Disclosure Agreement? Why is it important?

_____

_____

_____

_____

_____

_____

_____

6. What should the cover letter include?

_____

_____

_____

_____

_____

_____

_____

■ Activities 5.1

1. List the supporting documents that would be applicable to your plan.
2. The Investor Presentation—by BusinessPowerTools™—PowerPoint template is designed for larger businesses. Open this presentation in Biz-PlanBuilder and edit as much of the template as desired to better fit a small business venture either for your business, LogaTorial's, or a client's. Delete and/or add slides if desired. (You can also edit your results in Word. Click **File>Send** to>**Microsoft Word** and select the **Outline only** option and click **OK**.)
3. The sample nondisclosure agreement in the Plan Presentation Masters of BizPlanBuilder is geared toward a potential investor such as a venture capital firm. Assume you are handing your business plan to a potential key employee, a person you hope will join you as Vice President of Marketing in return for a small salary and some stock options with the potential of striking it rich when the company goes public in about five years. Modify the nondisclosure agreement to fit this situation. Consult with your instructor on how best to approach this adaptation.

Those who believe money can do everything are frequently
prepared to do everything for money.

—Anonymous

Funding Resources for Your Plan

While navigating your new or existing business on its intended road to success, there are many varied funding paths you can take. This section will help you conduct informed evaluations of capital in the right places, and early on, before your funding needs jeopardize your business. And it will show you where to find more valuable information and guidance resources in BizPlanBuilder and JIAN online. The BizPlanBuilder Resources Masters ⬧ Resources contains several kinds of documents—white papers, confidence builders, and even lists of hyperlinks—to help you focus on funding resources, from angels to bankers—and the kind of special "Zen" it takes to achieve that composure that shows you are responsible and capable of adding value to the money that banks and other kinds of lenders "need to see."

The insights presented here can give you leverage and advantage over someone else who may begin the process only when already desperate for immediate financial assistance.

■ Identifying Your Capital Needs

Identifying your capital needs and seeking the right source of financing for filling those needs can get confusing and complicated at times. You may have started in business as a specialist in a particular area of business marketing, sales, R&D or operations. Now as an owner or manager you need at least a general understanding of all aspects of business, especially appropriating and making efficient uses of funds.

The basis for your business may be a very sound concept, but funding new growth or maintaining existing growth can pose many challenges. Different types of capital requirements need different funding vehicles, all with different rules and steps similar in many ways to a game of Monopoly or chess. Growing a business most often requires more capital than is readily available from existing cash flow or from the resources of the founder(s). Conversely, obtaining too much capital or raising it too soon can also cause other problems for the business.

The first step in this search is to learn and understand the pros and cons of the various types of capital needed by your enterprise. Capital comes into your business in two ways: as Equity capital or as Debt capital.

Equity financing is the investment of the owner(s) in the company. It stays in the company for the life of the business (unless replaced by other equity) and is repaid only when and if there is a surplus in the liquidation of the business—after all creditors are paid. Usually getting new equity is very difficult, especially during the early stages of the business.

Debt financing, on the other hand, can come into the business in a variety of ways. It comes for a defined period of time and is paid back with some form of interest.

The financing of your business can be further classified as startup financing, which is usually equity, working capital financing, and growth financing. Startup financing is the financing to get the company to an operational level, including the costs of getting the first product(s) to market. This is best done with equity and long term loans or leases.

Working capital is required to drive the day-to-day operations of the business. In most businesses the operational needs vary during the year (seasonality, inventory buildup, etc.) and the working capital tides over the fluctuating expenses involved with doing the base business.

Growth capital is not tied to the yearly aspects of fueling the business. Rather, it is needed when the business is expanding or being changed in some significant and costly way that is expected to result in higher and increased cash flow. It is generally longer term than working capital and is paid back over a period of years from the profits of the business.

Knowing what type of capital your business will be needing will put you in a stronger position when evaluating how and where to seek your financing.

■ Narrowing the Search for Funds

Next you need to become familiar with the pros and cons of the various sources of financing and how each might cater to your specific capital needs. Are you an established business needing to buy fixed assets such as a new building or new equipment? Or do you need to add a new line of inventory to your stock? Are your needs for short-term money to help you through a seasonal cash crunch? If so, the typical source of financing for these kinds of needs is a traditional commercial bank.

If you are starting a new business and have sufficient collateral but need additional capital funds, the SBA loan program might be for you. For loans $150,000 and under, the Small Business Administration has eased documentation and collateral requirements to encourage and support small businesses with its SBALowDoc Program. The SBA also is encouraging women and minority-owned businesses with its new quota system. (See SBA Funding Programs in the following pages.)

However, if your proposed business is on the leading edge of technology, and there is a potential for substantial growth, venture capital might be the appropriate financing source. These types of funding are discussed later in this part. Knowing the specific needs of your business will help to significantly narrow the scope of your funding search.

To keep abreast of funding options for your business, network with industry colleagues and successful business leaders in your region, solicit the advice of financial experts, and read well-regarded financial publications.

Many entrepreneurs and investors are now also turning to online financing services, which are appearing with greater regularity. Some of these services attempt to match small businesses with investors, while others electronically post lists of companies seeking investors and then allow investors to examine the lists for companies of interest. Usually both the businesses and the investors pay fees to have access to this service.

The Web, too, must be monitored, too, for options. BizPlanBuilder provides and excellent starting point from its toolbar. Clicking the Find $$$ button will take you to a JIAN webpage that linked to funding resources such as the Venture Alliance and the National Venture Capital Association, and so on. There is also a hyperlink to VCgate, an online directory of venture capital, private equity, merchant banking, and other investment firms that provide funding. And, lastly, there is pertinent advice on how to recognize and avoid scams.

When you visit the Find $$$ websites, keep a sharp eye out for creative ways in which other successful businesses—especially ones like yours—are handling their funding. Follow up any leads for funding ideas that hold promise for your type of business. Most of all, don't get stuck in a rut of focusing on only one type of financing. Keep your options open. Hold several cards that can be played at the appropriate time for your business.

The following is a description of many of the options available for funding businesses in today's economy. The most commonly used funding sources are described for you more fully than the less-used, narrower in scope methods. For your convenience, the sources have been generally grouped into the following categories: Self Funding, Private Resources, and Commercial Funding.

■ Self Funding

Most businesses ventures (close to 90 percent) are begun with less than $100,000 and close to a third are begun with less than $10,000. This kind of money is usually available to the motivated entrepreneur by taking a close look at the personal resources at his or her disposal well in advance. Several of the most common self-funding methods are described here.

Personal Savings and Equity

This capital reflects the degree of motivation, commitment and belief of the founder in the enterprise. This type of investment also takes the shape of sweat equity, where individuals either donate their time or provide it at below market value to help the business get established.

Moonlighting

Many home-based businesses are begun while the founder is still working a regular job. The income from the job can both help support the owner during negative or low cash flow of the business set-up phase and it can provide working capital to augment the business's cash flow.

Home Equity Loans

This may be the fastest growing method of raising money for individuals. Banks generally are willing to lend up to 70 percent or more of a home's appraised value, minus any existing mortgage(s). For tax purposes, you can deduct interest on up to $100,000 of debt on home equity loans, regardless of how you use the money. You may also want to take advantage of the many kinds of refinancing options that make it possible for you to raise money with the value of your home.

Insurance Policies

Some entrepreneurs have been known to completely cash in their life insurance policies. Many insurance companies have, in recent years, liberalized their criteria for allowing policy holders to borrow against the value of their policy.

Tax-Deferred Retirement Accounts

Dipping into your tax-deferred retirement account can be a last resort for funding your business. This works best if you are more than 59½ years of age. While the money in your Individual Retirement Account or 401(k) plan is technically available to you, you'll need to pay a 10 percent early withdrawal penalty plus regular income tax on money you withdraw. It might be possible to get an unsecured loan on the strength of your retirement accounts. Although these accounts would not directly be pledged as collateral, the money could be withdrawn at a later date to repay the loan if it was required.

Credit Cards

"Pulling out the plastic" for fast funding of your business is more viable now than ever before. MasterCard or Visa card holders with good credit now often receive credit limits of $10,000 or more. Credit card interest rates on cash advances vary considerably—as do annual fees. This means it is wise to investigate getting the best deal you can when obtaining your credit cards. It may be advantageous to close out one or more of your high interest cards and transfer the balances to lower cost credit cards.

If you go this route, you need to be more than just your average "educated consumer." If your venture should fail, the credit card payments can place you in personal financial jeopardy. Learn as much as you can about the credit industry vis-à-vis small businesses. Consult such online credit card information providers as Cardweb.com. And remember, obtaining funds through credit cards costs much more than bank loans. If you do use your credit cards for business funding, pay them off in a timely manner. Paying only the minimum payments can extend interest for years without making much progress toward paying off the principal.

Bootstrapping

Often the best money to go after is the money that can be saved from the current costs and overhead of your ongoing business. The process of thoroughly searching through your operation for opportunities of savings and improved efficiencies will also allow you to learn more about the intricacies of your company, which will put you in a position to manage it better—a double return on your invested time and effort.

Customers

Certain types of businesses can require an advance deposit from customers, which quickly spurs cash flow. If you can encourage cash payments instead of giving customers credit, you avoid financing them. Similarly, you can also facilitate receiving cash quickly by granting cash discounts for early payments by customers. In any case, the more quickly your success has an impact on your suppliers and customers, the more likely they are to offer such deals.

Stock Purchases and Options to Employees

Your employees can be your partners in solving needs for capital at your company in a variety of ways. You can offer certain senior and trusted employees to become common stockholders by investing in a purchase of your company stock. Employees usually have limited discretionary funds for stock purchases, but every dollar counts, and employee dollars usually come with the motivation to help improve the results of the company, thus the value of their investment.

Common shareholders also have the right to have a say in the management of the company. Another possibility is to offer these employees nonvoting preferred shares of stock in return for their investment.

Employee Stock Ownership Plans

Companies can formally set up ESOPs (as they are called) to not only raise capital, but also raise employee morale and productivity. In a typical ESOP the employee is allowed, as determined by management, to purchase up to a certain amount of stock during a certain period of time. There are generally regulations about cashing in (redeeming) the stock if the employee should leave the company. An example might see an employee being able to have five percent or more of his or her weekly salary deducted for stock purchase after one year of employment.

■ Locating Private Resources

Just as it has in the past, reality suggests that the world of private investors, including friends, relatives, coworkers, wealthy acquaintances (angels) and various sophisticated individual investors, is a likely place to go to raise capital for your business. The total pool of all types of private investments in business is vast. For example, in 2004 the U.S. the venture capital industry invested approximately $21,004,400,000.[*] As huge as this pool of money is, the forms that individual private business investments take are diverse as is the creativity of the people making the deals.

---

[*] Source: National Venture Capital Association, "Industry Statistics," 2005.
<http://www.nvca.org>.

Choosing this private path leads to questions of how to find and inform a sufficient pool of potential investors about your need for private funding. Then, in exchange for the investors' money, what mechanism should be used to issue to them the documentation or securities that represent some equity or debt interest in your business? The key is *knowing* what aspects of deals are critical to your business and having multiple options available as you search for and enter into your funding negotiations.

Investment from Friends and Family

Next to personal savings, the second most popular source for startup capital is friends and family. Often, they may not be as worried about quick returns as other outside investors would be. There have been many success stories from investments of friends and family. There is also a high incidence of problems associated with this source.

Because the process of due diligence is often not carried out with family and friends, problems sometimes ensue. Thus, receiving capital from such a consenting, informed investor is often better than from a rich, unsophisticated relative or friend. Your relative or friend may not investigate your deal carefully and, should problems occur with the business and investment, your relationship with them may suffer.

A wise policy is to provide the same disclosure to a friend or relative that you would provide to most sophisticated investors. Resist the temptation to keep things loose and undocumented. Draw up the terms, conditions and payment schedule in writing for their signature and yours. Even if you receive a "friendship loan" at no or low interest, provide documentation in return. This is the smart, professional business approach that minimizes the potential down side of unstated assumptions and their implications. As a result of formalizing your deal, your relationship with your friends and family will have a much better chance of remaining intact.

Angels

▶ **Do It in BizPlanBuilder**

Check the other template libraries for resources to help you with investors.

In the Manage your Business library, there is an

Investor Game Plan

If you are a small business and you only need limited amounts of capital, seeking the type of private investor called an "angel" might be the best alternative. Hundreds of thousands of these angels invest billions of equity into small businesses each year. These people generally invest in sums well under $100,000, but sometimes you can get more by dealing with several "angels" at once, since they sometimes prefer to invest as a group.

Angels—a kind of person-to-person investor—have sometimes been called the "invisible" segment of the venture capital industry. Networking through trade associations, civic organizations, and your business community may lead you on the path to an interested angel. With individuals you have a tremendous amount of leeway in structuring the investment. You can structure it as debt or equity and vary the terms and repayment. Sources of personal investors go beyond family and friends.

A profile of the typical angel investor can vary, but here are some characteristic that are commonly found in the definitions of business writers:

- Income exceeds $100,000 and net worth in excess of $1,000,000

- 40–60 years old

- Previous successful entrepreneurial experience

- Expects to hold on the investment for up to five to seven years (but some angels wish to cash out after only a few years)

- Prefers to invest close to home—within one day's travel

- Enjoys advising the entrepreneur and likes to be part of the action

- Invests up to $150,000—but smaller sums are not unheard, especially when investing with other angels

- Refers deals to other private investors even if the angel has chosen not to invest

- Prefers companies and industries that are a "known quantity"

- Sources deals through referrals[*]

Previous or Present Employer

Your employer may not want to lose your abilities and contributions, should you decide to start your own business. There are situations where this employer can become your first major customer. This can be solidified with a purchase order if you are going to be providing manufactured goods, and also a specifically worded work-for-hire agreement if you are to provide services to your past employer.

In another situation, your employer may agree with you that it would be wise to spin off an idea of yours into a new company. Providing funds in this type of venture of yours may be a sound investment for the employer, who should already know the market, the competition and your abilities and motivation.

Individual Partners

This is a way to join forces with one or more individuals to expand the capabilities of the business. Like a marriage, the partners bring different, and hopefully complementary, resources to the business. For example, one may bring technical expertise, while the other may bring the primary financial resources. Another desirable match may be to team a person who has administrative abilities with a person who has strategic vision.

A partnership can be a way to get a business up and running while one or both partners still have other work or business commitments. It may also be effective in the early stages of business growth or in turnaround situations.

Corporate Partners

A trend that started in the 1990s and continues into the 2000s sees small businesses forming partnerships with larger corporations. Most Fortune 500 compa-

---

[*] Adapted from Ralph Kroman, "Partnering with Angel Investors," WeirFoulds LLP, 1991. <http://www.weirfoulds.com/publications/articles/angel.html>.

nies are now involved with these arrangements as a part of their corporate strategy. In this model, the larger corporation becomes a minority owner of the smaller company.

As a small business you receive the advantage of access to capital. You may also receive, as you grow, access to some of the resources of the larger company, such as distribution capabilities and product development opportunities that could act as formidable barriers to entry for potential competitors of yours. Your partner company gets into attractive markets and will share in your profits.

Strategic Alliances

In an effort to quickly put together a profitable project, it is becoming more commonplace to have two or more enterprises join forces for collaborative work. A popular book, *The Virtual Corporation*, by William H. Davidow and Michael S. Malone, touches upon this concept in detail. With businesses becoming more complex and global every day, and with increased emphasis on specialized knowledge and on fast new product development, partnerships are increasingly emerging among companies and entrepreneurs. The movie industry has modeled the concept of strategic alliances for decades. Diverse talent is sought and brought together for a common, defined project. After the movie is completed, many contributing elements to the production are quickly disbanded.

Private Foundations

With determination and the ability to prove that a "charitable" investment in your enterprise will have positive social impact, benefiting more than just you, finding funding from a private, nonprofit foundation is possible. While some foundations fund entrepreneurs directly, most foundations give money and support services to nonprofit organizations, which seek to accomplish the foundation's mission by coordinating and supervising the distribution of these resources in exchange for the specialized work needed.

Private Placements

In the United States, there are only two ways to legally offer (sell) the securities of your company to investors:

1. The transaction must either be registered with the Securities and Exchange Commission, as is done when a company "goes public" in the traditional sense.

2. Or it must be exempt from SEC registration, often referred to as a private placement or limited stock offering.

Due to the considerable legal requirements and the large commitment of time and money involved with a registered Wall Street public offering, many companies may not be ready to go public, and others may not ever want or need to do it. In recent times exempt offerings are becoming more viable alternatives for companies in search of early funding.

If your company is a viable candidate for offering securities to private investors via private placement, you must have prepared the proper documents you need to comply with federal and state securities laws and regulations. Upon completion of paperwork and proper filing, you'll need to identify potential investors, market your offering to them and, most importantly, track your results. By going through this process you will:

1. Be equipped to generally evaluate your fund-raising situation.

2. Determine where you may need help.

3. Become knowledgeable of current exempt offering issues and regulations.

4. Perform the necessary preparatory steps.

5. Generate proper documents to put into effect a Private Placement for your company.

Limited Partnerships

If you know who your investor(s) will be ahead of time, a limited partnership may be an easy, relatively fast and inexpensive way for you to create a business partnership. This form of raising money for business usually involves one general partner who represents the business owner or management team and several limited partners who remain generally silent and inactive in the operation of the partnership.

Emphasis in limited partnerships by investors has shifted away from tax write-offs toward yield and safety, with a renewed interest in them as a hard-asset component of balanced portfolios.

■ Tapping into Commercial and Government Funding

One of the greatest benefits of our free enterprise system of supply and demand is the vast network of diverse, targeted funding vehicles that has evolved. It has been fine tuned over recent decades to provide specific types of capital to different businesses in different industries and regions. The opportunities to turn business dreams into reality are in large part carried out through various channels of this vast, commercially based funding system.

Commercial Banks

In addition to lending money in various ways, banks also provide their business customers with various accounting, collection, payroll and bookkeeping-related services (for fees). These outside services are often less costly than doing it yourself . . . another way of minimizing your need for additional financing.

The Guarantee of Repayment

Because of the conservative nature of lending, a loan officer usually looks for two primary repayment sources plus collateral. The only way a bank can be repaid is with cash. The first source of repayment is the historical ability of a business to produce more cash than it uses. Profits plus depreciation do not equal the cash a business produces each year. Other factors like the collection of accounts receivable, the expansion of inventory, and the payment of accounts payable must also be considered. Bankers will also look at the personal credit history of the owner in many business situations.

As you have learned thus far in *BizPlanBuilder Express*, this is the kind of information you use to flesh out your business plan. It needs to be expressed there—in the plan—as well as the following issues that concern bankers.

The second source of repayment is the apparent ability of the business to produce enough cash in the future. A banker knows that past performance is no guarantee of future potential (think Eastern Airlines, Chrysler before Daimler-Chrysler, International Harvester, Enron, and, more recently Ford and General Motors). The banker will look to see how solidly the cash flow projections have been put together, how knowledgeable you are about the cash coming into your business and how it's being spent, and your ability to avoid a cash shortage.

Even if a business meets these two requirements, a good banker will still look for a third source: personal guarantees or collateral, anything you can show that is available as security for repayment of the debt. Examples of collateral are stocks and bonds, equipment, savings account passbooks, accounts receivable, or the cash value of life insurance policies. Remember, banks are not real estate brokers. They don't want to have to sell your property, they want cash.

Given the conservative nature of banking, those companies with established track records (this excludes new businesses) looking to finance expansion or seasonal changes in cash are the perfect candidates for bank loans. They have the proven ability of past performance, they are able to reasonably project the future and they usually have collateral. The sound business usually has the three repayment sources required by a bank.

Successfully Applying for a Loan

With a general understanding of how banks and bankers operate, how do you successfully apply for a loan? The best way is to prepare a complete loan package, which is comprised of forms that ask for must of the same information that you build into your business plan.

The first page of the loan package should list how much money you want to borrow, how long you want to borrow the money for, the rate of interest you expect to pay, how the money will be used (purpose) and a brief statement of why you need the money (cause). For example, you need to borrow $25,000 for inventory. That is the use or purpose of the loan. The cause is the addition of a new product line and the resulting sales growth.

The package should include a page or two history and description of the business. It should state when and where the business was opened, who the owners are, and how the business evolved to where it is today. It should discuss who your customers are and how you market to them. This section also includes a description of your products and services and a statement about your competition. The description of your competition should list their strengths and weaknesses and what sets you apart from them.

Next, you need to discuss your future goals and objectives for the company. This section will include in more detail how the borrowed money will be used and the effect on the company. Inclusive in this section is a set of budgets that will illustrate the future ability of your company to repay the note.

Lastly, you need to include copies of at least the last three years' financial statements and IRS tax returns for the business, your personal tax returns for the same period and your personal financial statement. This information may already be in the supporting documents of your business plan, created with the `Personal Financial Statement` template. If you are offering any type of collateral, a description of that should also be included.

SBA Funding Programs

The U.S. Small Business Administration has enjoyed a renaissance and is one of the leading resources for starting and succeeding with a small business. Congress created the U.S. Small Business Administration (SBA) in 1953 to help America's entrepreneurs form successful small enterprises. Today, SBA offices are set up in every state, the District of Columbia, the Virgin Islands, and Puerto Rico in order to offer financing, training and advocacy for small firms. The Agency also works with thousands of lending, educational and training institutions nationwide.

The SBA's Web site (**www.sba.gov**) shows this with resource links for startup kits, do-it-yourself research, workshops and online classrooms, training, counseling, patents and trademarks, shareware—and, of course, business plans.. For those small businesses looking for startup funds, the SBA might be the best approach. The SBA provides its broad-based Loan Guaranty Program as well as a variety of special financial programs.

SBA Loan Guaranty Program

The best approach for SBA financing is to find a commercial or savings bank that is a certified SBA lender. Although any bank can apply for an SBA guarantee, most do not have the appropriate staff or training to process the applications or monitor the loans according to SBA guidelines. However, those banks that are certified SBA lenders can usually get a response from the SBA in a matter of days.

The SBA can guarantee as much as 85 percent on loans of up to $150,000 and 75 percent on loans of more than $150,000. In most cases, the maximum guaranty is $1 million. There are higher loan limits for International Trade, defense-dependent small firms affected by defense reductions, and Certified Development Company loans. Although there is no specific break in the interest rate charged, one advantage for the borrower is the ability to repay the note over an extended period of time. The SBA generally caps rates at 2.25 to 2.75 points over prime, plus a fee equal to approximately two percent of the loan. Close to a quarter of SBA loans go to startup companies.

In order to qualify for the SBA guarantee, the borrower must first be considered credit worthy under normal lending guidelines. The SBA is not in the business of guaranteeing bad loans! Once the lending institution accepts the credit, it recommends it to the SBA. As traditional bank financing to small businesses has become increasingly difficult to obtain, the popularity of SBA loan programs has grown tremendously. In 2001, close to $10 billion of SBA loans were made to the private sector, a sum that is nearly 40 percent more than the levels seen in the early 1990s.

> **While SBA does offer some grant programs, these are generally designed to expand and enhance organizations that provide small business management, technical, or financial assistance. These grants generally support nonprofit organizations, intermediary lending institutions, and state and local governments. The bottom line is this: Uncle Sam funds a number of projects and institutions—such as the Women's Business Centers—to help your small business succeed**

Some of the the loan programs are well established now, such as the 7a Loan Guaranty, SBALowDoc, SBAExpress, SBA Export Express, Community Express, CDC–504 Loans, Pollution Control, and the Veteran and Micro-Loan programs. Others are specialized and designed around specific purposes, such as recovery assistance and loans for those small businesses in regions impacted by such disasters as 9/11 and Hurricane Katrina in 2005.

Typically, the SBA prefers to finance new businesses or the acquisition of existing businesses. It does not like to refinance existing debt and. in order to do so, the borrower must demonstrate a significant hardship caused by the existing debt relationship. The SBA does consider guaranteeing mortgage loans for buildings occupied by the business owner.

The SBA offers many services, such as the Small Business Development Centers and the Service Corps of Retired Executives (SCORE), to help entrepreneurs put together loan packages. Check these services out before turning to the professional "loan packagers." If you need professional assistance, ask your bank to recommend a loan packager. They charge around $1000 to $1500 to complete the volumes of paperwork. Look at the track record and ethical practices of anyone you consider.

The Small Business Development Centers are partially funded by the SBA and by state governments. Although not in the business of lending money for small business, this organization is an excellent source of information. They offer all kinds of continuing education courses and one-night seminars specifically for the business community. These courses are usually free or require only a minimal fee. The SBDC also offers free counseling. They will not write your business plan or find the best location for your business, but their corps of experienced counselors is usually a superb source of advice, guidance, and mentoring. The SBDC is organized on local levels and has offices at about four dozen universities and junior colleges. To locate an SBDC look in the phone book under the U.S. Government listings for the office nearest you.

Microlenders

In the 1990s and early 2000s microloans have become popular in areas where ready access to business funding has traditionally been limited. Microlender programs tend to be revolving funds offering a few hundred dollars to $35,000 loans. This money is usually provided at high market-rate interest and is often coupled with training and technical assistance to the qualifying entrepreneur.

Thus, this vehicle for funding should be used cautiously as a resource if traditional loan sources do not prove to be helpful.

The www.sba.gov Small Business Financing webpage is a great place to begin researching ways to finance your business with government and private funding.

The SBA has its own Microloan Program, which began in 1993. It bypasses banks and works through a network of community development corporations called "Microloan Intermediaries." These technical advisors include for-profit and nonprofit and are further divided into lenders and nonlenders. For more information, see the Micro-Loan Program webpage at **http://www.sba.gov/ financing/frmicro.html**.

Venture Capital

The NVCA defines venture capital as "money provided by professionals who invest alongside management in young, rapidly growing companies that have the potential to develop into significant economic contributors. Venture capital is an important source of equity for start-up companies."[*] Venture capital investing grew from small investment pool in the 1960s and early 1970s to a mainstream asset class by the 1990s. After a three year decline in the first part of the decade, venture capital investing rose to in 2004 and it appears that opportunities will continue to grow.

---

[*] Source: National Venture Capital Association, "The Venture Capital Industry—An Overview," 2005. <http://www.nvca.org>.

Venture capitalists are usually looking for high growth candidates in certain niches in which they specialize their expertise. A large portion of venture capital investments are poured into technology and health care companies. VCs (as they are called) assume relatively high risks. One-third of their investments are partial or total losses, a third are between break-even and two times cash on return, while the other third of VC investments realize returns of greater than two times. The big winners have to make up for all the losers and marginal performers.

Even if you do fit their narrow parameters, their money often comes with various strings, including specific performance requirements, legalities, and intrusion into your company's goals and operations. Typically, they want to see proprietary and protected technology (patented), opportunity for significant growth, a clear "exit/harvest strategy" (go public, be an acquisition, leveraged buyout or merged within 5 to 10 years, and so on.) and most importantly a cohesive, seasoned and committed management team. They bet as much on the jockeys as they do on the horse. That includes sometimes replacing jockeys—which could be you. They will want a comprehensive business plan, but it better grab their attention in the first couple of pages or else they'll toss it. These guys and gals play hardball, so you'd better be prepared to play their way. This is often a very narrow option not available to 99 percent of businesses.

Some of the most common ways to raise venture capital funding are described in the following paragraphs.

Venture Capital Funds

Venture capital usually refers to a fund or pool of money established for the sole purpose of making an equity investment in small, high-growth companies. The VC fund accepts and manages investments from individuals and invests that money in small companies with high growth prospects.

Investment Banking Firms

Venture capital is also raised occasionally by investment banking firms. Traditionally, investment bankers concentrate on investment in established, larger companies; however, they do invest in specific new ventures in emerging growth industries. They'll typically form a syndicate of investors for a qualifying venture proposal. Deals with investment banking firms can range in hundreds of thousands of dollars to several million.

Boutiques

A variation on investment banking firms is the investment "boutique." Boutiques operate on a smaller scale, aiming at local or regional companies who need capital in the low million range. They raise funding for ventures through private individuals, banks, finance companies, and investing their own capital.

Venture capitalists like businesses on the leading edge of technology or new industries. They like to see the potential for sales to at least double on an annual basis and the possibility of a multimillion-dollar industry being developed. The advantage of venture capital over bank loans (asset based lending) is that they don't have to be repaid. It is an equity investment.

The repayment does lead to a major concern of venture capitalists. Their investment is not permanent. They usually like to fund the company for five to ten years and then want to be bought out. They are not long term investors. Therefore, part of the initial offer must be the objective of going public or being purchased by a larger company. Either way, you must be able to prove that the fund will be able to find a ready market for their investment at some point in the intermediate future.

The venture capitalist is taking a large risk that your company will fail altogether or will not grow sufficiently so that they can sell their stock. For this risk, they require a substantial return on their investment. This return can be in the form of dividends during the growth phase or might be in the form of a substantial profit on the sale of the stock. Either way, expect the venture capitalist to want a big chunk of the business and a big return on his investment.

Going Public

For certain companies with proprietary products or unique services in "hot" industries, an Initial Public Offering (IPO) or selling shares to the public is an enticing yet expensive way to obtain large amounts of capital. This market was booming in the mid-1980s, then went into the doldrums after the major stock market setback in 1987. Through the 1990s IPOs returned to prominence again—and have done so again in the post-9/11 economy

On the positive side, going public is a way to obtain cash for significantly growing a business quickly. It is also a way for the CEO/owners to "cash out," to pay off debt and the stock option reward to key employees, and to attract top notch talent into your company. Achieving success after an IPO will help facilitate additional fund acquisition for equity increase or more favorable terms on future borrowing. Mergers and acquisitions may also be more easily accomplished with stock transactions instead of using cash.

Proceeding with an IPO is a major decision that requires much specialized expertise, 18 to 24 months to execute and significant expense. An investment banking company typically underwrites the deal and may collect from six to ten percent of the offering's gross proceeds. Legal and accounting fees often top $100,000 for an IPO, as can other printing and registration fees. Other downsides to an IPO are high levels of required disclosure of information to the government and to investors, some loss of owner's control and management flexibility, higher susceptibility to a takeover and short-term pressure on performance/dividend.

Franchising

In the United States, there are over a three-quarter of a million franchised outlets that account for over a $1 trillion of all retail sales. Internationally there may be over 250,000 more—with much of the growth in China, India, and in other rising economies. It has been a very fast growing phenomenon, especially during the last few decades. Franchising involves a franchisor who owns, produces, or distributes a particular product or service, who grants exclusive local distribution rights to a franchisee—that person or entity that agrees to certain standards of business and who provides a payment or royalties to the franchisor.

As a funding method it can be looked at from two directions: as a franchisor you can extend your existing business to multiple locations and areas; as a franchisee you can quickly start a new business or speed up the growth of your existing business. From both directions franchising involves using another person's or business's capital to mutually expand one's own business. In addition to funding benefits, both parties can grow because of standardized marketing, name, controls, and facilities. Each can benefit from the inherent economies of scale. As a franchisee you can view this situation as one that lessens the overall risk of getting into business.

The International Franchising Association provides in-depth information on franchising. There are a variety of books, periodicals and trade publications that list franchising opportunities and the issues surrounding them. Your local newspaper classifieds may be a good place to start looking for what may be available in your area.

Commercial Finance Companies

Commercial finance (or loan) companies have evolved out of large manufacturing companies that established subsidiary companies to finance the parent company's receivables. Many of these financing subsidiaries grew successfully to the point that they began using their surplus funds to provide similar services to other companies.

For companies who get turned down by commercial banks, commercial finance companies will often be more accommodating. Because these finance companies are willing to make loans to relatively high risk borrowers, their loan rates are generally higher than commercial banks and other sources. Credit lines usually run at prime rate plus an additional certain percentage and closing fee.

A revolving credit line is the most popular form of funding offered by commercial finance companies. They are almost exclusively secured lenders requiring collateral—and they usually advance up to 80 percent of accounts receivable or inventories. Some commercial finance companies are also involved with fixed asset financing and factoring discussed next.

Factoring Companies

Factoring is a method of receiving money as a loan based on your accounts receivables. The factoring company, in effect, buys your company's accounts receivable and then either provides money on the date invoices come due or advances money before the invoices come due.

Large factoring firms generally charge a commission of one to two percent of the total dollar volume of the invoices bought. If advancing funds, which usually are up to 80 percent of the value of the invoices, the factoring firm charges two to three percent above the prime rate. While factoring is relatively expensive, it is a way to generate needed cash in a hurry. The factoring companies are proficient at knowing the credit track record of your customers because they interface directly with them in collecting on their loans to you.

Leasing

Beginning in the late 1970s, leasing has grown to become a popular form of receiving funding by using your acquired assets as security. The trucking and railroad industries are good examples of businesses that rely on this method. Leases work best when the leased asset involved is usable for a long term, has value independent of use at your business and takes relatively little management time or effort if the item should be reacquired at the end of the lease or if you default on payments.

Leases can be arranged through many asset suppliers or through third-party companies that deal primarily with the financial aspects of the deal. In an operating lease situation, the leasing company owns the equipment and provides services such as repair and insurance. In a financial lease, you are responsible for the services while the lessor merely owns the equipment.

Veterans Administration Guaranteed Loans

As a benefit to honorably discharged veterans, the Veteran's Administration has long offered a small business loan guaranty program similar to the SBA Loan Guaranty Program. The Veteran's Administration will work with you to guarantee the majority of your loan in order to help your chances of loan approval through traditional lending avenues. Look in your phone book to locate the Veteran's Administration office closest to you.

■ Parting Tips

Recurring themes throughout Part 5 (and Part 4, too) have been about learning the financial needs within your company and also becoming aware of the various alternatives of financing that are available to you. Look at these issues early and often as you develop your business. Read, ask, look and listen. If having sufficient capital to grow your business stays high on your business priority list, the opportunities will be there for your benefit.

Be inquisitive and open minded, yet be cautious and safe. Check on both the institutions and people with whom you may be dealing. Know their track records during both the good times and bad times of their other customers. Know about second sources for any financing path you may intend to follow.

■ BizPlanBuildercise 5.3: Explore Funding Resource Advice

In this exercise you will locate the Resource files in BizPlanBuilder and select a Resource document to review.

1. Launch BizPlanBuilder if necessary and select the LogaTorial or your own business plan.

2. In the BizPlanBuilder Masters section of the Item List, locate the Resources library icon and expand the file tree as shown in the illustration below.

3. Right-click the **What Investors Look For** and select **Open**.

4. Review the Expert Comment and content of the What Investors Look For document.

5. List of the kinds of lenders and advice that best fits your business venture.

_____

_____

_____

_____

_____

_____

_____

_____

7. Close BizPlanBuilder if desired.

Optional Exercise. Open one or more other Resources documents. Examine them for relevance to your business venture.

■ Review Questions 5.2

1. a. What is startup financing?

_____

_____

   c. What are the three main capital components of startup financing?

_____

_____

_____

d. Would you expect to get them all from the same source of funding?

_____

_____

_____

2. a. What is the main source of funding for the vast majority (close to 90 percent) of businesses that are begun with less than $100,000?

_____

_____

_____

b. Why is this a popular method?

_____

_____

_____

3. a. What are some common private resources?

_____

_____

_____

_____

b. Why are private resources so important?

_____

_____

_____

_____

_____

4. What is a private placement of stock?

    _____

    _____

    _____

    _____

    _____

5. What is the SBA Loan Guaranty Program?

    _____

    _____

    _____

    _____

    _____

6. Does the SBA actually loan the funds? If not, who does and how does the SBA help?

    _____

    _____

    _____

    _____

    _____

7. Who or what are angels?

    _____

    _____

    _____

    _____

    _____

8. a. What type of companies are venture capital firms seeking?

_____

_____

_____

_____

   b. What level of risk are they generally willing to accept?

_____

_____

_____

_____

■ Activities 5.2

1. Throughout this text you have been using your potential business or role-playing ventures—or, in some cases, your current business—as an illustration in some of the exercises and activities. Now that you have done all of the underlying work for your business plan, what type of capital do you need—equity, debt, working or growth? How much of each? Considering all of the options covered in this chapter, which funding sources will you pursue and why?

2. Triad Distribution is a small warehouse operation in central Illinois with plans to establish a huge regional distribution center for gourmet and specialty food items. Triad would sell directly to grocery and discount supercenters, delivering the product with its own fleet of trucks. The one giant distribution center would be highly computerized and use robotics to select and pack orders. The center would be able to supply a 10 to 12 state area.

    Triad is working on a business plan. Initially $1 million will be needed to finance the continued study of the concept, draw up plans, and pursue customers and financing. Next Triad will need $40 million to fund the building and pay for software development. Most of the equipment and trucks will be leased, but another $2 million will be needed for deposits and down payments. In addition, working capital for inventory and payroll will need another $7 million.

    As an outside consultant to Triad, write a memo suggesting appropriate sources for these capital needs. Be specific as to which sources would be best for various needs and why

    OR

    You are a consultant to E-Lit, an online distributor of books that can be downloaded and played in an MP3 player or Apple IPod. Which SBA program and resources would you recommend to the owner of E-Lit? She wants to expand her business by financing a new Web presence with a new online shopping interface tied to her inventory and a new advertising campaign of banner ads.

She needs about $100,000 to finance her marketing expansion.

Consult the SBA website and research your answer before turning it into a written memo.

You win not by chance, but by preparation.
—Roger Maris

Appendix A: Preplanning Resources

The Preplanning Masters in BizPlanBuilder provide a number of activity documents to help you focus on where to begin with your business plan. It is the place to begin if you are new to BizPlanBuilder or if you have upgraded from an earlier version. The About BizPlanBuilder document lists the important changes and major enhancements that have been introduced into the latest version of this business plan software. (You will also want to see the discussion that follows in the next appendix, Postplan Operations: Resources for Managing Your Business. There are other documents and templates that can be used for the preplanning phase of your business venture.)

Scroll down in the Item list and then expand and view the Pre-Planning Masters templates in the file tree.

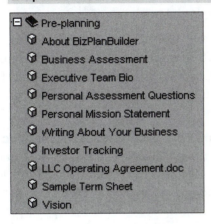

When you expand the Pre-planning library icon , you will see several document templates. The **About BizPlanBuilder** surveys the program's features, benefits, and latest innovations. Other templates are selected and highlighted in the following paragraphs.

The **Personal Assessment Questions** is a template that is divided into a set of questions in which you can develop your personal reasons for owning a business. The questions themselves are divided into the following categories:

- Your Motivation—What are/were your personal reasons for starting your own business?

- Your Interests and Experience

- Personal Considerations

- Factors for Success—What need will your business fill?

Because it is just as hard to cold call on your intentions as it is cold calling on a potential client or investor, this template provides sample responses that you can customize the same you customize the templates in the other BizPlanBuilder Masters.

The responses to the **Business Assessment** template's questions help you to structure your thoughts, ideas, and inspiration in a way that supports keeping focused on what you want your business to be. Like the Personal Assessment, its companion document, the Business Assessment is divided into questions and sample responses that you shape into your own. The following categories of questions and answers are covered:

- Your Market

- Your Business

- Finances

Both of these question-and-answer documents may elicit no responses to certain kinds of questions—such as how much money you need. However, you need to know where the knowledge gaps are before you begin. You need to know what you don't know.

A "think piece" related to the previous templates is the developing a **Personal Mission Statement** document, which features a number of applicable passages by Stephen Covey. Once you have your Personal Mission Statement in hand, applying the same approach to developing a mission statement for your company will be easy.

You probably have some kind of vision for your business. Otherwise, you would not be writing a business plan. The **Vision** document is not a template but a discussion of vision excerpted from *First Things First* by Stephen R. Covey, A. Roger Merrill, and Rebecca R. Merrill. A solid vision, supported by a clear mission statement, helps you implement principle-based values and business practices that fulfill your stated company mission.

The **Writing About Your Business** discussion document provides you with ways to rationalize and articulate your business plan. It poses, for example, a scenario where you

> Imagine a friend coming to you with an idea and wanting to borrow $10,000 . . . What would *you* want to know? How will this business make money? Who's going to buy the product or service? What is your friend going to do with your $10,000? When will you get it back, and how much money will you make?

In addition to considering your own value to your business venture, you may also want to sketch out the other stakeholders in your business plan-in-progress: your management team. The **Executive Team Bio** template provides a quick way to formalize the education and experience that you will have to bring off your business's success.

If everything seems under control, you're just not going fast enough.

—*Mario Andretti*

Appendix B: Postplan Operations: Resources for Managing Your Business

BizPlanBuilder's usefulness does not end with the finished business plan. The Manage Your Business Masters ◆ Manage Your Business is a library file of different postplan templates and documents that you can use. There are even templates that can be included in your business plan, as in the case of the Private Offering Cover Disclaimer.

Below is a survey of selected business management documents that highlights their utility to your business plan.

The Manage Your Business Masters file tree.

```
─ ◆ Manage Your Business
    📦 Application For Business Credit
    📦 Business Startup Checklist
    📦 Commercial Lease
    📦 Due Diligence Checklist
    📦 Free Publicity
    📦 Independent Contractor Agreement
    📦 Investor Game Plan
    📦 Invite to Board of Directors
    📦 Invite to Board of Advisors
    📦 Lehman Formula Calculator
    📦 Management Notebook
    📦 Private Offering Disclaimer
    📦 Product Feedback Survey
    📦 Proceeds of Sale of Business
    📦 Service Feedback Survey
    📦 Space Requirements Planning
    📦 Trademark Instructions
    📦 Trademark Overview
```

The **Investor Game Plan** is as much a preplanning document as it is a postplanning document for an established business contemplating expansion. Use its thoughts and questions to develop a game plan for approaching investors for your business. This document also gives you a time table for the different kinds of investment stages:

- Seed investments: 0–9 months for Concept and Planning

- First-round financing: 6–18 months for Product Development

- Second-round financing: 12–24 months for Market Development

- Bridge financing: 24 months to achieve Sustained Growth

- Later Rounds for a liquidity event such as acquisition/buyout or IPO

Another document that can be used in the preplanning state is the **Business Startup Checklist**. It begins with a check-off for the Business Plan. But it also includes such important considerations as licensing issues, filing a DBA, leasing arrangements and the like—all of which should be in process if financing is impending and you need "to hit the ground running." The **Trademark Instructions**, **Trademark Overview**, **Commercial Lease**, and **Space Requirement Planning** documents are also designed for optimizing pre- and postplanning business considerations.

The **Independent Contractor Agreement** template is for a business that relies on temporary and part-time freelance workers who manage their own hours and must agree to paying their own taxes and benefits. This agreement also includes the standard disclaimer from the software manufacturer. So you should seek legal counsel before actually putting it into use. You may also want to consult your federal, state, and local tax laws as well, since freelance workers who make all of their income from one vendor may not qualify as an independent contractor.

Usually the success of your business, especially if it's a sole proprietorship, is spread by word of mouth. This is one kind of free publicity. The other is supplied by JIAN, Inc., whose editors will speak to its software customers about their experience using JIAN products like BizPlanBuilder. These editors want stories about real customers with real business issues—and how they successfully addressed those issues. This can lead to free publicity for your business through articles published in business, software/computing, and in-flight magazines; trade publications; and business sections of local and national newspapers. To learn about this advantage, consult the **Free Publicity** document. JIAN will also sometimes post customer success stories and photos at its Web site. (The Small Business Administration also posts similar success stories at its Web site. So, if your business benefited from an SBA loan, you should let the SBA know.)

The **Due Diligence Checklist** is designed for companies that require a comprehensive disclosure of the business, its status in the marketplace, and financial condition before an impending sale of the business entity or for some similar change in its structure, such as the death or resignation of a partner. The information garnered from the checklist would be used for various kinds of reports and legal documentation. The checklist might also be used as an internal evaluation tool, and a centralized repository for essential information about the company. Since certain information you supply in the checklist is of a highly sensitive, proprietary nature, it should be kept in a safe place. (Note the legal disclaimer that holds the software manufacturer harmless. You should always obtain your own legal counsel when preparing such a document as the Due Diligence Checklist.)

Another template that will help you in selling a business is the **Proceeds of Sale of Business** spreadsheet, which can be customized to analyze what your profit would be. The calculations that you make with this spreadsheet should be checked by your CPA.

Once you are in business, you will need to establish credit with suppliers and other firms. The **Application for Business Credit** is a standard template form that you can freely adapt and then fax or e-mail to vendors as needed.

A handy spreadsheet is also included in the Business Management Masters: a **Lehman Formula Calculator** template. This is a compensation formula developed by Lehman Brothers for investment banking services. The structure is as follows:

- 5% of the first million dollars involved in the transaction

- 4% of the second million

- 3% of the third million

- 2% of the fourth million

- 1% of everything thereafter (above $4 million)

Because of inflation, investment bankers often seek some multiple of the original Lehman formula and various adaptations exist.

You can track the goals of sales, management, marketing, product development, administration as well as other parts of your business in the **Management Notebook**. BizPlanBuilder recommends using a three-ring binder to organize this essential management information that you can turn to in an instant. And you can modify the headings to suit your business's type and structure.

Another kind of assessment is tailored specifically for service and product development. Use either the **Service** or **Product Feedback Surveys** to conduct field tests. The templates can be given to beta testers to assure confidentiality.

Trademarks are considered an asset and as such they should be protected. The **Trademark Instructions** and **Trademark Overview** provide a quick how-to guide for trademark application with the the U.S. Patent and Trademark Office.

Often you just have to rely on your intuition.
—Bill Gates

Appendix C: System Requirements

BizPlanBuilder® Express has been designed for the **interactive Windows version of BizPlanBuilder 10**. To use this version, your computer must be running Windows ME, 2000, or XP (including Server 2003).

You must also have installed and running on your computer Microsoft Office 2000, XP, or 2003. Your computer must have the following minimum system requirements:

- A PC-compatible computer

- One of the specified Windows operating systems

- One of the specified versions of the Microsoft Office suite or standalone versions of Microsoft Word and Microsoft Excel

- 256MB of RAM

- 60MB of free hard disk space

- A CD-ROM device if installing BizPlanBuilder from a CD-ROM

- Internet access and a browser to download MIDAS and BizPlanBuilder installation files.

- Internet Access to use Internet resources available on the BizPlanBuilder toolbar

- A mouse or similar point-and-click device

If you need online support, click the Support button ⊙ in the BizPlanbuilder toolbar or visit the support site at **http://www.jian.com/** and click the Support link in the navigation bar.

■ Installing the Interactive Version of BizPlanBuilder

Simply insert the BizPlanBuilder CD-ROM and follow the onscreen instructions. It's that easy. You will first install the MIDAS document assembly engine and then the BizPlanBuilder database.

■ Moving the Business Plan Folder from the Desktop

For computer labs and other classroom settings, the default placement of the Business Plan folder may not be desirable. Do not move this folder or any of its subfolders using such methods as Send To or drag and drop in Windows Explorer. The BizPlanBuilder database needs to be properly updated if the folder is moved because features of the program—plan variables, other users, permissions, etc.—have specific locations. To avoid errors, perform the following steps:

1. Open and sign into BizPlanBuilder with the path pointing to the default "BusinessPlan" folder on your desktop.

2. In the BizPlanBuilder menu bar, click **File** and **Copy Selected Plans**.

3. You will see a list of plans/projects in the currently active folder. (The one you logged into when you started this session with BizPlanBuilder)

4. Check the box(es) for the plans you want to copy in the Copy Plans dialog box shown below.

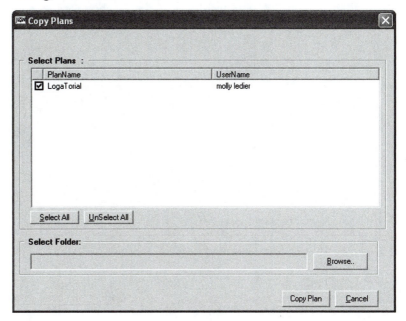

5. Click **Browse** and select the folder location where you want to move your /plan(s).

6. Click **Copy Plan**.

7. Close BizPlanBuilder.

8. When you open BizPlanBuilder again, before signing in, click `Change..` and select the new folder location made in step 5.

9. Click **OK**.

10. Click `Sign In` and select the desired plan.

■ Using the Template Version of BizPlanBuilder: For Macintosh Users

Macintosh users should be running OS9 or OS10 and Microsoft Office 2001 or later. BizPlanBuilder for Macintosh is a collection of Word and Excel templates that contain the same content as the Windows version of BizPlanBuilder. Unlike the Windows version, with its MIDAS document assembly system, the content has been formatted directly into complete word-processing and spreadsheet plan templates that you can easily edit.

The BizPlanBuilder for Macintosh ships as a compressed file and requires Unstuffit. It installs as a folder containing the documents organized in subfolders, with an "About" page to introduce the JIAN business tool you have chosen.. For more information, vist **http://www.jian.com/**, click **Business Plan Software**, and under :Learn More click **Macintosh Version**.

.

The subjects reported that with word-processing programs they not only wrote more freely but also planned less.

—from an early study, ca. 1991

Appendix D: Using Microsoft Word and Excel

This course has been written with the assumption that you have at least a working knowledge of operating the Microsoft Word word processing and the Microsoft Excel spreadsheet applications for Windows. If you are new to these powerful productivity programs, the authors of *BizPlanBuilder Express* recommend that you seek training to enjoy all of the features of the Interactive version of BizPlanBuilder, which achieves its best results when used with Microsoft Word and Excel.

There are two ways to accomplish this training. If your school offers courses in using Word and Excel, you should consider enrolling in them. You can also self-train yourself to learn the basics of Word and Excel. Whatever route you take, not only will your ability to work in the Document pane of BizPlanBuilder be easy, your new skills will also be transferable to the needs of your business venture and to your career as a whole.

■ Training for Microsoft Office

For those who like to learn on their own, visit a favorite bookstore or shop online to find the many Microsoft Office introductory computer tutorials that Microsoft Press, Course Technology, and other companies publish. You can also take courses to learn Word and Excel.

If you are currently enrolled in college, consider taking one of the elective computer training courses offered for learning Microsoft Office. Ask your instructor for more information or consult your university's computer lab or IT department for course offerings.

Microsoft Training (**http://www.microsoft.com/learning/training/**) is the starting point for seeking more comprehensive introductory learning that can lead to specialist certification. This will give you skills that you can use for more than just working in BizPlanBuilder—consider it an investment in your business operations.

> *The further back you can look,*
> *the farther forward you are likely to see.*
>
> — *Winston Churchill*

Bibliography

The following is a list of suggested readings that have inspired this book and that will inspire you in writing your business plan and managing your business venture. A list of online resources follows.

- William Alarid, *Money Sources for Small Businesses.* Santa Maria, CA: Puma Publishing Company, 1991.

- C. Gordon Bell with John E. McNamara, *High-Tech Ventures, The Guide for Entrepreneurial Success.* Reading, MA: Addison-Wesley, 1991.

- Gustav Berle, *SBA Hotline Answer Book.* New York: John Wiley & Sons, Inc., 1992.

- Kenneth Blanchard, Patricia Zigarmi, and Drea Zigarmi, Leadership and the One-Minute Manager: Increasing Effectiveness through Situational Leadership. New York: William Morrow, 1985.

- Zenas Block and Ian C. MacMillan, Corporate Venturing: Creating New Businesses Within the Firm. Boston: Harvard Business School Press, 1995.

- Laurie Blum, *The Complete Guide to Getting a Grant.* New York: Poseidon Press, 1993.

- Laurie Blum, *Free Money for Small Businesses and Entrepreneurs.* New York: John Wiley & Sons, Inc., 1992.

- Stephen C. Brandt, *Entrepreneuring, The Ten Commandments for Building a Growth Company.* New York: NAL Penguin Inc., 1982.

- William B. Bygrave, *The Portable MBA in Entrepreneurship.* New York: John Wiley & Sons, Inc., 1990.

- Lawrence Chimerine, Robert F. Cushman, and Howard D. Ross, *Handbook for Raising Capital: Financing Alternatives for Emerging and Growing Businesses.* Homewood, IL: Dow Jones–Irwin, 1987.

- William H. Davidow and Michael S. Malone, *The Virtual Corporation.* New York: HarperBusiness, 1992.

- Peter Drucker, *Innovation and Entrepreneurship: Practices and Principles.* New York: Harper Business, 1993.

- Drew Field, *Take Your Company Public! The Entrepreneur's Guide to Alternative Capital Sources.* New York: New York Institute of Finance, 1991.

- Burke Franklin, *Business Black Belt,* Mill Valley, CA: JIAN Tools for Sales, Inc., 2000.

- Roger Fritz, *Nobody Gets Rich Working for Somebody Else, An Entrepreneur's Guide.* New York: Dodd, Mead & Company, Inc., 1987.

- Charles L. Frost and Eugene E. Valdez, *How to Prepare a Bank Financing Proposal For Your Business (The Way a Banker Would). Study Guide and Workbook.* Valdez, Frost & Co, Business Finance Consultants, 1992.

- Robert J. Gaston, *Finding Private Venture Capital for Your Firm: A Complete Guide.* New York: John Wiley & Sons, Inc., 1989.

- Paul Gompers and Josh Lerner, *The Venture Capital Cycle.* Cambridge, MA: MIT Press, 1999.

- Tom Hopkins, *How to Master the Art of Selling.* Scottsdale, AZ: Champion Press, 1982.

- Lee Iacocca with Sonny Kleinfield, *Talking Straight.* Boston, MA: G.K Hall, 1989.

- Seymour Jones, M. Bruce Cohen, and Victor V. Coppola, *The Coopers & Lybrand Guide to Growing Your Business.* New York: John Wiley & Sons, Inc., 1988.

- Gregory F. Kishel and Patricia Gunter Kishel, *How to Start, Run, and Stay in Business.* New York: John Wiley & Sons, Inc., 1993.

- Randy Komisar, *The Monk and the Riddle: The Art of Creating a Life While Making a Living.* Boston: Harvard Business School, 2000.

- James M. Kouzes and Barry Z. Posner, *The Leadership Challenge! How to Get Extraordinary Things Done in Organizations.* San Francisco: Jossey Bass, 1987.

- Joseph C. Krallinger and Karsten G. Hellebust, *Strategic Planning Workbook.* New York: John Wiley & Sons, Inc., 1989, 1993.

- Michael LeBoeuf, *The Greatest Management Principle in the World.* New York: Putnam, 1985.

- Christopher R. Malburg, *All-In-One Business Planning Guide.* Holbrook, MA: Bob Adams, Inc., 1994.

- Christopher R. Malburg, *Business Plans to Manage Day-to-Day Operations.* New York: John Wiley & Sons, Inc., 1993.

- Joseph Mancuso, *How to Start, Finance and Manage Your Own Small Business.* Englewood Cliffs, NJ: Prentice-Hall, Inc., 1984.

- Rita Gunther McGrath and Ian C. MacMillan, *The Entrepreneurial Mindset: Strategies for Continuously Creating Opportunity in an Age of Uncertainty.* Boston: Harvard Business School Press, 2000.

- Mark H. McCormack, *What They Don't Teach You at Harvard Business School.* Toronto, New York: Bantam: 1984.

- Ronald E. Merrill and Henry D. Sedgwick, *The New Venture Handbook.* New York: AMACOM, 1993.

- National Venture Capital Association, *2005 Venture Capital Yearbook,* Arlington, VA: NVCA Press, 2005.

- David Ogilvy, *Ogilvy on Advertising.* New York: Vintage Books, 1985.

- Thomas J. O'Malia, The Entrepreneurial Journey: The Road to Starting Your Own Venture, second edition, Cincinnati: South-Western College Publishing, 2002.

- Gifford Pinchot and Ron Pellman, *Intrapreneuring in Action: A Handbook for Business Innovation.* San Francisco: Berrett-Koehler Publishers, 1999.

- Stephen M. Pollan and Mark Levine, *The Field Guide to Starting a Business.* New York: Simon & Schuster, 1990.

- Al Ries and Jack Trout, *Marketing Warfare.* New York: McGraw Hill, 1986.

- Al Ries and Jack Trout, *Positioning: The Battle for Your Mind.* New York: McGraw Hill, 1986.

- Jerry M. Rosenberg, *The Investor's Dictionary.* New York: John Wiley & Sons, Inc., 1986.

- W. Keith Schilit, *The Entrepreneur's Guide to Preparing a Winning Business Plan and Raising Capital.* Englewood Cliffs, NJ: Prentice-Hall, Inc., a division of Simon & Schuster, 1990.

- Andrew J. Sherman, *One Step Ahead, the Legal Aspects of Business Growth.* New York: AMACOM, 1990.

■ Online Source/Resource Supplement

- The Small Business School, the series on PBS, WorldNet, and the Web, **http://smallbusinessschool.org**

- Lycos Small Business resource, **http://business.lycos.com**

- The Patent Café, a resource for product development, **http://www.patentcafe.com**

- National Venture Capital Association, a resource for understanding the venture capital industry, **http://www.nvca.org/**

- Bizdevjournal, a resource for marketing business development, **http://bizdevjournal.com/index.htm**

Index